The Art of Selling

For Business Colleges
High Schools of Commerce
Y. M. C. A. Classes and
Private Students

By

ARTHUR FREDERICK SHELDON

Formulator of the Science of Business
Building and Editor of "The Business
Philosopher"

1911
THE SHELDON UNIVERSITY PRESS
LIBERTYVILLE, ILLINOIS

COPYRIGHT 1911
THE SHELDON UNIVERSITY PRESS

Entered at Stationers' Hall
London, England

ALL RIGHTS RESERVED

In the interest of creating a more extensive selection of rare historical book reprints, we have chosen to reproduce this title even though it may possibly have occasional imperfections such as missing and blurred pages, missing text, poor pictures, markings, dark backgrounds and other reproduction issues beyond our control. Because this work is culturally important, we have made it available as a part of our commitment to protecting, preserving and promoting the world's literature. Thank you for your understanding.

CONTENTS

A...GENERAL PRINCIPLES OF SELLING.................. 9

Lesson *1*—Everyone has Something to Sell.............. 11
Lesson *2*—Salesmanship and Success.................. 13
Lesson *3*—Service: The Source of Profit................ 16
Lesson *4*—Service: The Source of Profit (*Concluded*).... 18
Lesson *5*—What is Profit?........................... 20
Lesson *6*—What is Service?.......................... 23
Lesson *7*—The Four Factors of a Sales Transaction....... 25
Lesson *8*—The Analysis of a Sale..................... 28
Lesson *9*—The Analysis of a Sale (*Concluded*).......... 30
Lesson *10*—How to Become a Salesman................ 32
Lesson *11*—How to Become a Salesman (*Concluded*).... 35

B...THE FOUR CLASSES OF SALESMEN.................. 37

Lesson *12*—Retail, Wholesale, Specialty and Promotion.... 39

C...PRACTICAL LESSONS IN RETAIL MERCHANDISING...... 43

Lesson *13*—The Right Viewpoint...................... 45
Lesson *14*—Salesmen Versus Order Takers.............. 48
Lesson *15*—Mental and Moral Discipline................ 51
Lesson *16*—Difficulties 55
Lesson *17*—The Harm of Negative Suggestions.......... 59
Lesson *18*—Positive Suggestion 62
Lesson *19*—Analyze Your Goods...................... 65
Lesson *20*—A Specimen Selling Talk................... 68
Lesson *21*—Answering Objections..................... 72

D...WHOLESALE SELLING 75

Lesson *22*—Preparing For a Journey................... 77
Lesson *23*—Technical Knowledge of the Goods........... 79
Lesson *24*—Getting an Interview...................... 82
Lesson *25*—The Tactics of Selling..................... 85
Lesson *26*—The Salesman's "News" 88
Lesson *27*—Almost Persuaded 91
Lesson *28*—The Salesman's Catechism................. 93
Lesson *29*—The Struggle With Competition............. 95
Lesson *30*—Pointers 98

226637

CONTENTS—Continued

E...PRACTICAL LESSONS IN SPECIALTY SELLING..........101

Lesson 31—On Specialty Selling........................103
Lesson 32—The Importance of Selecting the Right Article..105
Lesson 33—How to Analyze the Article..................107
Lesson 34—Thinking Out a Selling Talk.................111
Lesson 35—Geography for Specialty Salesmen............116
Lesson 36—Practical Hints 122

F...PROMOTION SALESMANSHIP........................127

Lesson 37—Promotion and Salesmanship.................129
Lesson 38—In Business For Yourself....................134

G...WRITTEN SALESMANSHIP 137

Lesson 39—The Theory of Written Salesmanship..........139
Lesson 40—What is a Selling Letter?....................142
Lesson 41—The Arguments and How to Arrange Them....145
Lesson 42—Effective English 150
Lesson 43—On Answering Inquiries......................154
Lesson 44—Letters of Complaint and How to Answer Them.158
Lesson 45—Follow Up Letters..........................162
Lesson 46—Selling Your Services by Letter..............165
Lesson 47—Collecting Accounts 168
Lesson 48—"Don'ts" For Office Salesmen................172

H...SELLING BY ADVERTISEMENT.......................175

Lesson 49—Salesmanship and Advertising................177

I...CONCLUDING SURVEY 179

Lesson 50—Suggestions For Further Study...............181

PREFACE

FOR a number of years now my whole time and energies have been consumed in expounding the Science of Salesmanship, and I have been compelled to turn a deaf ear to requests from many quarters for a text-book suitable to students in High Schools of Commerce, Business Colleges and other centers of commercial education, although I was not unaware of the compliment thus bestowed on me.

During my travels about the country in 1910-1911 I found a book was needed on *The Art of Selling*—a theme quite distinct from the Science of Salesmanship—and the following pages stand for my attempt to supply that need.

Men who can sell are in great demand. Not long ago I counted the advertisements in a Sunday issue of the Chicago *Tribune* and found 111 firms were needing the services of salesmen. A field of labor so wide, offering remuneration up to $10,000 a year, is one for which a course of school or college study is emphatically necessary, not as a complete preparation, but as an introduction to the great theme of salesmanship.

Being a practical salesman myself, as well as a teacher of the science, it is no credit to me that by force of circumstances I should have the advantage of knowing the subject from all points of view; but still this advantage is ultimately to the benefit of the student, and he will find in the lessons of this book an exposition of the principles which apply to salesmen of every type. I look forward to the day when selling will figure a good deal more conspicuously than it does now in the curricula of schools and colleges; for when it is realized that every one has something to sell, education will take steps to provide means for teaching the mental law of sale.

I have prepared a small hand-book for the use of teachers who conduct classes where the *Art of Selling* is the text, and copies can be obtained by applying direct to me. This applies also to private students who are unable to attend classes.

A. F. S.

A
GENERAL PRINCIPLES OF SELLING

LESSON ONE

Every One Has Something to Sell

IF you were to draw up a list of different kinds of men and women engaged in earning a living, you would find several characteristics common to the whole number; and chief among these characteristics is the fact that every one has *something to sell.*

Let us draw up a brief list to test this statement:
1. A commercial traveller.
2. A bookkeeper.
3. A stenographer.
4. A laborer.
5. A doctor.
6. A lawyer.

You could greatly increase this catalogue of employments, trades and professions until it included every line of useful effort, but that would not in the least alter the truth that each person obtains an income by selling something to the purchasing public.

The commercial traveller is a salesman in a special sense—that is, he goes from place to place, exhibiting samples and soliciting orders in a direct manner by personal appeal.

The bookkeeper, however, sells his *knowledge* of keeping accounts, his skill, and a certain part of his time; the stenographer sells his (or her) skill in shorthand and typewriting; and the laborer disposes of his brawn and muscle for a weekly wage.

The doctor sells his skill in medicine and surgery for a fee; and the lawyer, on the same basis of a fixed rate of payment, offers his acquaintance with law to those who feel the need of such a purchase.

Thus it is true to say that every one has something to sell. Even the man who has retired from business altogether is no exception. He sells the use of his capital to those who would borrow, and lives on the interest that accrues.

But we who are still in active work do not sell our goods in

THE ART OF SELLING

the same way. The commercial traveller, for instance, is selling all the time by direct persuasion of individual buyers representing themselves or large corporations.

On the other hand, the bookkeeper, the stenographer and the laborer have only one actual sale to record, namely, the bargain or agreement with their employers to deliver their services at certain wages; but in a real sense they are selling their services every working day.

The doctor and the lawyer do not, as a rule, appeal to the public for employment—it is considered unprofessional to do so—but indirectly they use, as we shall see later, many of the arts of the salesman in an endeavor to secure patronage.

It is important you should grasp firmly the theme of this first lesson. You may not know as yet what goods you yourself are going to offer the public, but you can study the goods of others. They may be selling pumps or poetry, lard or literature, medicine or sewing-machines, legal skill or pulpit orations. However different the product, the fact remains that it is produced for sale.

So begin to observe this vast market of miscellaneous commodities, and do not forget to notice the many different ways in which men and women place their goods before the public; when you think of your future, remember that your income will depend on the quality of your goods and the skill with which you can sell them to an employer.

EXERCISES

A. REVIEW QUESTIONS:
  (1) What is the most common characteristic of all persons actively engaged in business?
  (2) Is a retired man an exception to the rule?
  (3) How does a commercial traveller differ, as a salesman, from a doctor and a bookkeeper?

B. QUESTIONS FOR WRITTEN ANSWERS:
  (1) Draw up a list of five occupations other than those given in the lesson, and show how they, in spite of real differences, stand for "something to sell."
  (2) Reply to the objection that "a man living on a pension has nothing to sell."

LESSON TWO

SALESMANSHIP AND SUCCESS

IF it be true that we all have something to sell, it is equally true that, to be successful, we must know how to sell it. This means that we must have the ability to find an increasing number of permanent and profitable patrons.

There are many people in the world who have high quality goods to dispose of, but they fail because they cannot sell them. They do not understand the science of salesmanship, and more than half the failures of life have their origin in this lack of power to market goods at a profit. Whichever way we turn we find illustrations of this fact. Let us take

(1) A bookkeeper;
(2) A preacher;
(3) A lawyer;
(4) A business corporation.

The bookkeeper has had, we will suppose, the best of training in all kinds of accounts; consequently he has a good deal of most useful knowledge to sell to a prospective employer. But he is an inefficient man—he cannot market his abilities. When he approaches an employer his talk about himself is a mumble-jumble. Even when he does get a position, after a lot of waiting, he can't get a "raise" in salary because he relapses into bad penmanship occasionally, or becomes careless in dress. This is another form of bad salesmanship.

The preacher may have a profound knowledge of human nature and the Bible, but on account of personal mannerisms and the habit of forgetting faces and engagements, he loses every chance of a continued and successful pastorate. He is a poor salesman of his magnificent abilities, and declining years will find him without a pulpit or a platform.

It is just the same with a lawyer who knows the law but cannot plead in the courts, because he has never become proficient in the art of speech. His competitor, with less knowledge but effective expression, neglected no opportunity and now reaps a rich harvest of clients and dollars.

Nor is the business corporation on a different footing. A dozen men may decide to form a company to put a new reaper on the market; they may organize a fine executive department, with good finance and producing departments to match; but, unless they study how to sell their reapers, all the other arrangements can have little or no result.

Clearly, then, it is one thing to have something good to sell and quite another thing to know how to sell it to advantage. This is why the study of salesmanship is so important to everybody, and especially to those who have not yet begun business life in earnest.

Soon you may yourself be offering for sale your knowledge and skill in office routine, or some other commodity, and you will find that success in life depends on the facility with which good goods are disposed of. The goods may be bookkeeping, typewriting, stenography, agricultural produce, sermons, hardware, sonnets, machinery, magazine articles or anything else. Much depends on their quality and on the public demand, and much depends on your ability to effect a sale.

So look around you and observe the manner in which men and women are trying to sell at a profit. Why do some succeed without difficulty, and why do others seem to fail, although they may be honest and industrious? Is it not because the former, consciously or unconsciously, know and apply the principles of salesmanship and the others do not? I think it is, and hope to make the statement good in the lessons that are to follow.

Meanwhile give your mind to the fact that "Every successful man is necessarily a good salesman." And salesmanship is the science which reveals the true relationship between buyer and seller. What that relationship is will be dealt with in the lessons that follow.

EXERCISES

A. QUESTIONS FOR REVIEW:

(1) "Every one has something to sell." What follows an acceptance of this statement?

(2) In this respect is a minister of a church on the same level with a merchant?
(3) Why is the study of salesmanship important?

B. QUESTIONS FOR WRITTEN ANSWERS:
(1) Supply a list of four occupations other than those stated in the lesson, and show how inefficient salesmanship leads to failure.
(2) Explain the importance of a good selling department in a large clothing factory.

LESSON THREE

SERVICE: THE SOURCE OF PROFIT

WE have now learned two great truths about business. One is that we all have something to sell; the other is that we must learn how to sell it to advantage.

Let us pause a moment to ask a question:

Why do we sell goods to other people?

The usual answer is, "Because we want to make a profit, and thus earn a living for ourselves and those dependent on us."

This is true, as far as it goes, but it does not go far enough. In business we all aim at making a profit, but there is only one right way of accomplishing that end, whilst there are many ways that are mischievous and fatal.

In these lessons it is my object to define and illustrate the right relationship between the buyer and the seller. Only by fully appreciating this relationship can you secure large or numerous profits in your undertakings.

In olden times trade was regarded as an occupation unworthy of an educated man and a gentleman. Such a man had a prescribed code of honor, and if he sinned he suffered. But for the trades there was no such code. On the contrary, the Roman law countenanced sharp practices as between buyer and seller—one of its maxims was *caveat emptor,* which means "let the buyer beware."

Many business men of all nations are still in bondage to the old idea which aims at profits—*somehow*. I have underlined that word because it describes the vague conceptions of so many people we meet. They know they want a margin of profit, but they have only a confused idea as to the best way of getting it, continuously, and in increasing quantities.

Talk with men in Chicago, New York, Paris, London or Berlin, and in reply to your question, "What are you in business for?" they will say, "To make money." True, but how? Too often their idea is simply a quick and effective means of transferring the cash in other people's pockets to their own. They think of their own enrichment first; the customer's benefit has little thought bestowed upon it. They try to *exploit* him instead of *serving* him.

Now the one fault with all methods of money-making that infringe the true relationship between buyer and seller is that they do not sufficiently consider the buyer's wishes. Those people who make the largest fortunes in trade are the people who give most thought to the needs of the public and to the best means of *serving* them. Those employees who draw the largest salaries are the men whose *services* are most valuable to their corporations.

Thus we see that true salesmanship, the disposing of any kind of goods at a profit to an ever-increasing number of patrons, is the science of *service*. Grasp that thought firmly and never let go.

EXERCISES

A. QUESTIONS FOR REVIEW:
   (1) What answer is usually given to the question, "Why do we sell goods to other people?" Wherein is the answer defective?
   (2) What did the Roman law say to the buyer?
   (3) How do profits come from service?

B. QUESTIONS FOR WRITTEN ANSWERS:
   (1) State in your own words, very briefly, the false attitude which many sellers take up in regard to the buyer's interests.
   (2) "The desire for big profits is responsible for much dishonesty in business." Illustrate this statement.

LESSON FOUR

SERVICE: THE SOURCE OF PROFIT *(Concluded)*

IN Lesson Three we considered business mainly from the viewpoint of the seller, as a man who wished to sell his goods at a profit. We found that true salesmanship was a service rendered to the buyer.

Now the buyer has a viewpoint, too, and we ought to look at a sales transaction through *his* eyes. When he parts with his money for goods—a railroad ticket, a bunch of flowers, a pair of trousers, or a loaf of bread—he expects to receive an equivalent of the sum expended. If he does not, he is naturally dissatisfied, and adopts means of spending his dollars to better advantage.

Note this carefully: that however keen the sellers of to-day are on making money, the buyer himself is keen on dealing only with those who serve him best. Think of the millions of people who every day must spend money in buying the necessities of life. What they want is not a seller who exploits their needs and thinks of nothing but seizing large profits by persuading customers to make purchases that will turn out to be disappointing. Customers go here and there looking for the best values at a fair price. In a word, they are in search of a seller who will serve them better than any other.

The keynote of the success of the late Marshall Field was service, and he was the father of the "goods returnable if not satisfactory and money refunded" idea. John Wanamaker once said to me (I do not quote his exact words): "If my institution can serve the public better than any other institution, then the public will be persuaded to make a beaten path to my door."

These testimonies to the truth I am trying to make plain are worth pondering, for they come from institutions ranking among the greatest in the world—businesses supplying the needs of the public with satisfaction to both parties in the transaction.

Contrast this method with the methods referred to in the last lesson. The kind of salesmanship that is most profitable does not seek to make money on the *anyhow* system. *That* plan may succeed for part of the time, but not for all the time. The salesmanship which seeks to serve is the real profit-bringer, because every buyer, without exception, is anxious to deal with the seller whose chief object is to give his customers satisfaction.

Men and women, with money in their purses, read the advertisements in the papers, scrutinize the store windows, compare prices and discuss values, the treatment accorded—and to what end? Just to find out who is the best salesman—that is, who will serve them with the articles they want in the best way, including price, quality, attention, etc.

So it comes to this, that there are millions of people in the world who are on the watch for the best sellers; and, as we know already, the best seller is the man who serves the public best. Once more, then, we see that service spells success.

In the next lesson I shall try to explain in detail what service really means.

EXERCISES

A. QUESTIONS FOR REVIEW:
  (1) What is the secret of the success of great businesses such as Field's and Wanamaker's?
  (2) What kind of seller does the buyer wish to deal with?
  (3) What is profit obtained on the *anyhow* plan?

B. QUESTIONS FOR WRITTEN ANSWERS:
  (1) Mention two large businesses which have become prosperous on the basis of service.
  (2) "Honesty is the best policy." Comment on this proverb in the light of Lesson IV.

LESSON FIVE

WHAT IS PROFIT?

IN the preceding lessons I have had a good deal to say about *profit* and selling one's goods to *advantage*. I purpose now to ask and answer the question, "What is profit?"

It may be defined as the difference between the total cost of anything and the total amount received in excess of the cost when it is disposed of.

Examine this definition carefully. Whether it is service that one is selling, or merchandise, or any other thing, from the viewpoint of profit, it is not the bulk of money received that is important. It is the difference between the total cost and the total amount received in excess of the cost that constitutes the *advantage* to the seller.

Take two illustrations: A merchant says, "I can buy this article for one dollar. I can sell it for two dollars. If I sell a million, I make a million dollars profit." This is false logic and has caused thousands of failures. The cost was *not* one dollar; it should include a portion of the charges coming under rent, taxes, salaries, and general office expenses. Consequently, instead of making a million dollars' profit on the sale of one million articles, he would make much less than that, for the other charges, plus the first cost, would run the total cost up to anything from $1.25 to $2.00, or even more.

Again, suppose you have been engaged as private secretary to the president of a new corporation at a salary of $125.00 per month. You want to figure out what you can save. Technically this would not be your profit, but the method I am about to deal with illustrates the same principle. You hastily calculate the cost of your car-fares, the cost of your clothes, and your living expenses. You decide, just as hastily, that you can save $5.00 a month. But you have forgotten to include the amount of your insurance premiums, your library subscription, and a number of other items.

When these are deducted, your five dollars' profit probably dwindles down to three dollars.

In any method of arriving at what money is "left over" when the deal is finished, all charges must be entered.

Profit is the difference between *total cost* and *total receipts* in excess of the cost.

The question now arises: What is it that regulates the size of a profit? In other words, why are some large, some moderate, and some small?

To discuss this in all its bearings would take more space than I can afford, but I affirm that the usual answer of "buying cheap and selling dear" is radically defective.

I do not say a man may not buy real estate for an insignificant sum and sell it for a fortune; but I do say in ordinary business it is an opportunity that does not happen frequently. And why?

Because competition is the great regulator of prices. There are so many people, in almost every line, engaged in competing for public patronage that huge profits obtained by "buying cheap and selling dear" are few and far between. Large profits are no doubt the rule with firms who make contracts for building bridges, only one of which they may sell in a year, but such an exception is easily understood.

In modern business the big dividends of a prosperous concern do not arise out of handsome returns on single articles, but on the accumulated small returns on a large number of articles. What the merchant wants, therefore, is a crowd of buyers who will make a vast number of purchases; and he can get buyers only by *serving* them. In this way it becomes evident once more that service is the true and only source of profit, which is further proof of the fact that in the business world all roads lead to service.[1]

EXERCISES

A. QUESTIONS FOR REVIEW:
  (1) How would you define profit?
  (2) Illustrate your answer from the case of an employer.

---

[1] There is an extended treatment of the subject in Lesson XIV of the Science of Business-building, pp. 20-21.

(3) What is wrong with the policy of "buying cheap and selling dear?"

B. QUESTIONS FOR WRITTEN ANSWERS:
  (1) How do you arrive at the amount you can save out of your salary?
  (2) "Lines of business that are altogether new yield larger profits than those which are old." Has this anything to to do with competition?

LESSON SIX

What is Service?

I HAVE had occasion to use this word Service a good many times, and although you may have a fairly clear idea as to its meaning, I think it will be wise to analyze it a little more closely than we have done hitherto.

Some confusion is certain to arise in a few minds about the uses of the word in ordinary conversation. For instance, you know a restaurant where the food is good but the service bad—that is, you have to wait a long time for your luncheon or dinner after you have given your order. You know a store where the merchandise is of high quality but the delivery service is slow—that is, you order an article on Monday and have to wait until Tuesday afternoon before you get it, although it was promised for Monday evening. This kind of service is only a small fraction of what the word means as we use it in reference to salesmanship.

Occasionally a student will stumble over the objection that "to render service implies being a *servant*." Rightly understood, that is just what a seller ought to be—the servant of the customer. Instead of suggesting degradation it suggests exaltation.

You remember the words of Christ: "He who would be greatest among you, let him be your servant." In that passage we have a great business principle, and if you will apply it to successful men of all grades, you will see how true it is.

But let us try to formulate a definition of Service. There are two parties in every sales transaction—the customer and the seller. The customer has a need to be satisfied; he wants food, or clothing, or a watch, or a walking-stick. The seller has these articles in his store and is anxious to supply the customer's need. The sale takes place. Perhaps a watch was the article purchased. The *manner* of disposing of the watch may have been pleasant or otherwise; when the customer gets home the watch may have stopped, or it may be keeping good time; the seller may have made a large profit or a small one; he may be pleased or displeased; he may have tricked his customer and lied to him, or he may have rendered a good equivalent for the money paid.

All these things may have happened, but service, as understood in these pages, means that in such a case the customer shall receive a good watch, worth the money he paid for it, and that the manner of selling it shall develop confidence in him by reason of courteous treatment and of honesty in describing the article. Good service requires that He shall leave the establishment with the feeling that he will go there again.

On the side of the seller it requires that he shall do all he can to engender satisfaction and confidence, and that the transaction shall yield him a fair profit.

Service is, therefore, that form of exchange where the profit of the seller is matched by the complete satisfaction of the customer.

EXERCISES

A. QUESTIONS FOR REVIEW:
   (1) Mention some popular uses of the word Service.
   (2) Is a business man a *servant?* If so, how?
   (3) Define Service.

B. QUESTIONS FOR WRITTEN ANSWERS:
   (1) Show how courtesy is an element in true service.
   (2) Reply to the objection that, as it is impossible to satisfy every customer, complete satisfaction is not an attainable ideal.

LESSON SEVEN

THE FOUR FACTORS OF A SALES TRANSACTION

SALESMANSHIP may be defined as "the power to persuade people to purchase product at a profit to the seller and to the service of the customer."

If you will examine this definition, you will find it contains four factors: (1) the sale itself, (2) the salesman, (3) the customer, (4) the goods.

Every possible aspect of a sales transaction comes under one of those headings. There are no exceptions. Try to find one and you will be disappointed.

If, for instance, you imagine that the cost of freight from one place to another is not included in the four-fold division, I reply that this is an item directly concerned with the *goods,* and has not a little to do with the *sale* itself.

If you think it is difficult to find a place for honesty and other virtues in the scheme, you will discover that the need of right principles runs through the whole; it is required in the sale, in the salesman, in the customer, and in the goods.

At first the four factors mentioned seem so simple and so easily remembered that the student may conclude there is little more to learn about them, but he will see later into how many sections they unexpectedly and yet naturally divide themselves. For instance, take the sale itself. Here we have quite a large field of inquiry.

Allow me to illustrate what I mean: You get into conversation with a man in the car about insurance. He turns out to be an agent, and at the end of half an hour's journey he has convinced you of the wisdom of immediate protection; the older you become the heavier the yearly premiums you will have to pay. So you write your name on the dotted line and take the first step towards buying a policy.

Now there is apparently nothing profound about this action. It looks like simplicity itself. But just think for a moment of the mental stages through which your mind passed. In the first place, you would say that the agent "got you to think about the matter." When you had done that long enough you felt it might be a good thing to act on his suggestion; and after further talk you decided to sign the application form.

Now, this *thinking, feeling,* and *action* enter into every sale. You were probably not conscious of them as you talked with the man in the car, but they occurred all the same. Some of the lessons to follow will deal with them in detail and they are sure to interest you.

The second factor in salesmanship is the salesman. Why was he so anxious to sell you a policy, and why did he succeed? Those are bigger questions than you may think they are. They involve answers that embrace his knowledge of insurance, his knowledge of you, and his knowledge of himself.

He might know insurance from A to Z, but if he did not know human nature, he would often fail to effect a sale. Even complete knowledge is not everything; there must be ability to *apply* that knowledge. This is where the third factor comes in— the customer.

He calls for prolonged and careful study; and when I say "he," I mean both sexes. The salesman must know how to approach men and women; and to do this he must be able to recognize their outstanding characteristics at a glance. They determine the manner of introducing his proposition and how he will press his arguments home.

The last factor is the goods. To secure satisfaction in the mind of the customer (and hence repeated orders) is the aim of the seller; and he cannot do this unless he has good goods and can show other people wherein their goodness consists. Bad goods will spoil everything else in the art of selling. Even good goods will often remain unsold, if the salesman is deficient in his knowledge of their merits or in his power of stating them.

Before leaving this lesson be certain you have memorized the four factors in the order given, and that you know the importance of each.

EXERCISES

A. QUESTIONS FOR REVIEW:
  (1) What are the four factors of salesmanship? Begin with the fourth and proceed to the first.
  (2) Do they include a virtue like punctuality?
  (3) What stages did the mind of a customer pass through to whom an agent sold an insurance policy?

B. QUESTIONS FOR WRITTEN ANSWERS:
  (1) Under which of the four factors would you include questions pertaining to profits?
  (2) One schoolboy (Jim) sells another schoolboy (Tommy) a pocket-knife for ten cents. Assuming that Jim does not (as often happens) exaggerate the virtues of the knife, describe the four factors as they apply to this transaction.

LESSON EIGHT

THE ANALYSIS OF A SALE

IN order to illustrate the workings of the customer's mind when he makes a purchase, I will suppose you are a stenographer just engaged by a large corporation in Chicago. From a hundred applicants you were one of four chosen and asked to call at the office. *You* were the seller; the *manager* was the customer; the goods were your *services*.

Now in selling goods the first thing to aim at is to obtain *favorable attention*. When you wrote a well-worded and well written application, stating your qualifications for the vacant position, you took the first step towards securing this favorable attention; and when you presented yourself at the office, neatly dressed and with senses and mind alert, you turned it into *interest*. So far all is clear.

The Manager looked into your record, compared it with that of the other applicants and perhaps tested your gifts.

Finding you were a shade better than the other men, he began to *desire* your services, and after thinking the matter over, he *decided* to engage you at the salary offered in the advertisement.

If you do your duty, the sale will end in *permanent satisfaction*.

Note these successive steps in the process of a selling transaction:

1. Favorable attention.
2. Interest.
3. Desire.
4. Action.
5. Permanent satisfaction.

The second step depends on the first; the third on the second; and so on to the end. If you had written a careless letter in the first instance, saying you could write "shortand" and knew some "Frensh," you would have made it impossible to obtain favorable attention. Even if you had written a telling letter, but presented yourself at the office with your tie creeping up over your collar and your general appearance unkempt, favorable attention would not have ripened into interest. Indeed, you might get so far as to arouse the manager's *desire* to engage you, and yet stop short at *action,* because he discovered a blemish in your career.

The same mental procedure is observable in selling any class of goods from mowing-machines to umbrellas. When I have lost several expensive umbrellas and a dealer I know offers me something serviceable that is very cheap, he gets my *favorable attention* at once, because if a stranger "borrows" this new article, I shall not feel the loss so severely. I examine the umbrella. It works well and the material appears to be substantial. I am now *interested* and almost immediately the *desire* to have one is awakened in me. I fold up the umbrella to see how it looks in that condition, and as its appearance satisfies my critical eye I take *action* and make the purchase. Should that umbrella wear well, the transaction will be one of *permanent satisfaction.*

There are, then, five mental states through which a customer's mind passes when he makes a purchase. He is not always conscious of them, and sometimes the transaction from the first to the last is instantaneous—like the boy who no sooner sees chocolate than he decides to buy some.

EXERCISES

A. QUESTIONS FOR REVIEW:
- (1) Name the mental states of a sale, beginning at No. 1 and going on to No. 5, and at No. 5 proceeding backwards to No. 1.
- (2) In what way are these states dependent one on another?
- (3) Does the difference in the nature of the thing sold affect the mental operations involved? Give reasons.

B. QUESTIONS FOR WRITTEN ANSWERS:
- (1) Describe a sale which fulfills the five-fold requirement of a successful transaction as outlined in the lesson.
- (2) May a sale justify your answer satisfy four of the conditions and fail in the fifth?

LESSON NINE

THE ANALYSIS OF A SALE *(Concluded)*

IN the previous lesson we analyzed a sale from the viewpoint of what must happen, mentally, to the customer in order that he should make a purchase.

I want now to reverse the picture and consider what should *not* happen. You will remember the five mental stages dealt with, and over against them I will place their opposites. The meaning of the contrast will be made plain later on.

POSITIVE	NEGATIVE
1. Favorable attention.	1. Unfavorable attention.
2. Interest.	2. Indifference.
3. Desire.	3. Disgust.
4. Action.	4. Repulsion.
5. Permanent satisfaction.	5. No sale.

Suppose I am in need of some collars and go out to find a store where I can buy them. The city is new to me. I have not been in it before. At last I notice a store with haberdashery displayed. I inspect the windows and find some collars suspended loosely on a wire. The window-dressing is bad throughout, and the display offers no attraction; but as I am in a hurry and cannot wait to find another store, I enter and make known my wants. The inside is not more prepossessing than the outside. There is no neatness and no order, thus creating *unfavorable attention*. The salesman is careless in his manner of showing me his goods, and I begin to blame myself for patronizing him. In spite of my hurry I am now quite *indifferent* as to whether I buy or not, partly because the goods are inferior and partly because I get the impression it does not matter whether I take them or not. At last the salesman shows some impatience. I had asked to see another brand of collar, and he muttered to himself as he went to the end of the store to find them. This *disgusts* me not a little, and when I see the collars are very old stock, and of a shape not now worn, I *decide not to buy.* Thus my mind has passed through the five negative mental stages, just as before, when I was buying an umbrella, it passed through the five positive mental stages. You will see how much depends on the creating of confidence, not only after a sale, by satisfying a customer, but before the sale and during its procedure. Confidence may be said to permeate every function of the law of sale.

Now, the reason why I have, at length, drawn your attention to this matter is because I wish to show how a sale contains elements that answer to the faculties of the mind.

In every mind there are three powers, classified as knowing, feeling and willing. *Attention* has to do with the knowing power; *interest* and *desire* have to do with feeling power; and *action* has to do with the willing power.

The great problem of salesmanship is so to master this fact that the customer, realizing his best interests are being served, is persuaded to make a purchase because you follow the right method. You do not try to make him take action before you have stimulated his desire; and you do not try to create desire until you have secured his interest.

EXERCISES

A. QUESTIONS FOR REVIEW:
  (1) What are the negatives of interest, action and desire?
  (2) Classify the three powers of mind in relation to the five mental transitions through which a customer's mind passes when making a purchase.
  (3) Why is the seller wise in obeying the mental law of sale?

B. QUESTIONS FOR WRITTEN ANSWERS:
  (1) Imagine you visit a store and meet with a poor salesman who fails to suggest anything besides the article you asked for. Write a brief account of the transaction.
  (2) Describe an attempted sale where the salesman makes the mistake of disobeying the law of sale.

LESSON TEN

How to Become a Salesman

I F you reflect a moment, you will see that all the foregoing lessons are explanations of the facts involved in the art of selling: they tell us *what the salesman's task is*.

With this lesson we start on a new road. It leads us to practical issues, because the time has come to consider what kind of training the salesman needs for his task. Up to now the lessons have centered in salesmanship itself. We must begin to show *how the salesman is educated*.

Educated? Yes. I use that word deliberately, for the statement that salesmen are *born*, not made, is easily misunderstood. I have heard it used with such dogmatic emphasis that I marvelled to think it was necessary for a "born" salesman to learn anything at all, even the names of his customers! The truth, as always, lies between two extremes. There is no salesman so born to his duties that he can dispense with a knowledge of the goods, or so independent of experience that practice teaches him nothing he did not know. More than others he can profit by a system of training, for this will double his earning powers by giving strength to his native liking for salesmanship. On the other hand, there are some, students and scholars for instance, whose temperaments are alien to selling in any shape or form, and nobody would claim such men could be made into salesmen. But that the average young man of business, with ambition, and ready for hard work, can never be a salesman unless he is "born" to it, as Tennyson was "born" to poetry, is absurd. I do not say every young man would accomplish the *same* success, but I see no reason why success in some degree should not be his, after he has finished his course of instruction.

The popular minister of a church might fail altogether, if he tried to sell combs and hair-brushes; the tactful doctor who can charm a group of patients, earning their undying confidence, would not succeed as a smart dry-goods clerk, and yet all these men are salesmen who are trained by the desire to excel and by the discipline of experience.

We are sellers—every one of us, and we have to learn *how* to sell, so that, whilst it is true that a few men have less to learn than others, all salesmen have something to learn. Shakespeare sold plays to his own profit and the satisfaction of the public; but genius though he was, he had to learn a few things about writing plays, as Prof. Dowden has pointed out.

What then has the salesman to learn in order to render the service which leads to the biggest profits? Turn back to Lesson seven on "The Four Factors of a Sales Transaction." It is there stated that they are the sale, the salesman, the customer and the goods.

The task before us, therefore, is to know these four with an ever-growing intimacy. Do not run away with the idea you can know them once and have done with it! Think of the amount of study needed to become a doctor, a lawyer or an accountant. They spend years in mastering physiology, law or figures.

Now, modern business is no exception to the rule—that is, if you wish to become a fully qualified man, you must give time to patient study. Trade used to be considered below the professions in rank, but in these days we teach that all men, without distinction, are salesmen either of goods, or knowledge, or skill or services.

Hence, whatever you intend to sell in the future, there are four subjects which must engage your attention. They are:

1. Self-knowledge.
2. Knowledge of the goods.
3. Knowledge of the customer.
4. An application of this knowledge, to the end of focussing mental agreement.

Note how the word knowledge is to the fore. Salesmanship is really *knowledge* skilfully applied. In the next lesson I shall pursue this topic further.

EXERCISES

A. QUESTIONS FOR REVIEW:
   (1) What is the reply to be made to the assertion that salesmen are born not made?
   (2) Are there men with greater natural ability for salesmanship than others? Give reasons.
   (3) If we all have something to sell, is there any difference between a trade and a profession? Why?

B. QUESTIONS FOR WRITTEN ANSWERS:
   (1) A doctor has to study, among other things, physiology, anatomy, medicine and surgery. What subjects would you place over against these as constituting the studies of a salesman?
   (2) "Mere book knowledge is of no avail." Comment on this passage in the light of the last paragraph in the foregoing lesson.

LESSON ELEVEN

How to Become a Salesman (*Concluded*)

IT may have surprised you to learn that in order to attain the profits of service you have to study the subjects enumerated in the list. I want to show you why it is necessary to know yourself, your goods, and your customer—and how to apply that knowledge.

It is necessary to know yourself because you have in you a number of success qualities, and you ought to know how to develop them, not by mere rule of thumb, but on scientific methods.

For instance, the work of salesmanship makes a certain demand on your physical powers. Unless you have an adequate knowledge of the laws of health, and of the best means of developing, using and conserving physical energy, you are in danger of falling sick at the moment when it is absolutely necessary you should be at your post.

Similarly you have mental powers which call for the same treatment. Success demands *ability* to think deeply and accurately, to remember unfailingly, and to imagine creatively. It demands *reliability* born of right feelings, such as loyalty, courage, faith and honesty. It demands the correct *action* born of the trained will. This is true because in business the best mentality wins.

It is necessary to know your goods because you cannot convince a buyer that they will be of service to him, unless you can explain them in detail, showing their nature and use. You cannot expect an order for safety-razors from a man who blindly believes in the old sort of thing, unless you can argue clearly the points of the new article. But to know your goods means more than this. It means a real understanding of business methods—advertising, cost accounts, and every item in the technique of manufacturing and selling.

It is necessary to know your customers because human nature exists in so many varieties that *one* method of approaching a buyer would not sell sufficient goods to pay expenses. You must know how to recognize and handle all these varieties of men and women, so as to effect a large number of sales and accumulate profits in proportion.

Some of this necessary knowledge will come from the formal study of human nature—and a good deal will arise out of experience. It is a supreme commercial advantage to be able to identify characteristics when we see them and to change our selling tactics accordingly.

But knowledge to be successful must be applied, and you must learn how to do that. Science is *knowing;* art is *doing*. You acquire the knowledge of all the facts that come under the head of the sale, the goods, and the customer, in order that you may make that knowledge practical in concrete deeds—in sales. In other words, focus mental agreement by bringing about favorable attention, interest, desire, action, confidence, and satisfaction in the mind of the buyer. Unless you can *sell,* you are not a salesman.

Persuasion is an art whose basis lies in service; you combine a number of knowledge items about your goods, yourself, and the buyer in such a way as to prove you are bestowing a benefit upon him in return for a specified sum.

The importance of applied knowledge is now clearly evident, and so far from being a dry study, it is one of the most fascinating you could undertake. Besides, it is the way to success in one of its many forms, and you do not intend to be a failure.

EXERCISES

A. QUESTIONS FOR REVIEW:
   (1) Why is it necessary to know yourself in order to be successful?
   (2) How does an intimate knowledge of your goods help you?
   (3) In what way is ability to judge character of service?

B. QUESTIONS FOR WRITTEN ANSWERS:
   (1) What is the difference, speaking broadly, between *science* and *art?*
   (2) Show how a real salesman must be a man of knowledge and a man of deeds.

B

THE FOUR CLASSES OF SALESMANSHIP

LESSON TWELVE

THE FOUR CLASSES OF SALESMANSHIP WHOLESALE, RETAIL, SPECIALTY AND PROMOTION

IT is customary to divide salesmanship into three classes: wholesale, retail and specialty selling; but I have added a fourth, because it represents a section that ought to be included in the classification—namely, promotion. It stands for the sale of an interest in a business, usually in the form of stock or shares, and, as a vast number of such sales are made every year, no treatment of salesmanship can afford to ignore them. The promoter of an enterprise is a salesman of unusual parts, as I shall try to show later on.

The wholesale salesman, as the name plainly indicates, represents a house which does business with retail dealers by supplying goods in large quantities. This fact naturally determines the list of buyers, for only men who buy to sell again can order goods in bulk. The wholesale salesman on entering a city knows to a man the possible outlets for his goods, whereas the specialty salesman, who may be offering a set of books, or a pianola, can form only a vague notion as to the number of customers who are likely to patronize him. Every house contains readers, and most houses have a piano; so from that point of view each specialty man might reasonably suppose that the possible market was represented by the number of houses. Experience tells him, however, that many people are content to read the newspapers and magazines—books are not in their line; and the other salesman, knowing that pianolas are expensive, cannot expect to sell a piano-player to every owner of a piano. Both men, on approaching a city, are therefore somewhat in the dark as to the amount of business they may be able to do. They have to hustle around and find out.

But the wholesale man, the man who is seeking a big order

for shoes, or something else, knows there are perhaps only three places of call for him, and it is to his interest to make those calls, sell what he can, and hurry off to the next city.

The retail salesman is in a position quite different from the others. The customer comes to him; he does not go to the customer, although he may advertise in a way to attract his attention. The retailer stands behind his counter to serve, and if a real salesman, not merely an order-taker, he will see to it that he renders the customer every possible service.

But all four types of salesmen obey the same law and work for the same end. The end is to effect a sale, and the law is the mental law of sale: they attract attention, awaken interest, arouse desire, and obtain a decision to buy.

The question has been asked: Ought a man to confine his attention to one type of salesmanship and train himself exclusively for that? Or ought he to be educated in the general principles of salesmanship, so that he can at will apply himself with ease to any one of the four?

The versatility implied in the last question is too vast for any one man to attain. It would be unreasonable to expect a salesman to turn his attention from wholesale work to specialties, and from specialties to retail, and from retail to promoting. To sell automobiles requires considerable technical knowledge, not only of one machine but of all competing machines, and this cannot be obtained in a brief period. Such a man could not at will become a salesman in a dry-goods store any more than the dry-goods clerk could turn out to sell automobiles.

Nevertheless, the chances of life are so uncertain that it is wise to prepare for eventualities by studying salesmanship in all its branches—not only in technical applications, but in its foundation principles. The men who travel, that is, the wholesale and specialty men have certain features of work common to both, and these I shall try to outline in the lessons to come: the retail man is a man apart, and his duties give his salesmanship another point of view. But all three, the promoter making a fourth, are sellers, and selling is an art we can study as applied to the whole group.

Thus, the plan to be followed is, learn the art of selling as it applies to every salesman, but learn it as it is applied to one business in particular.

EXERCISES

A. REVIEW QUESTIONS:
    (1) How is a wholesale salesman different from a specialty salesman, and how is a retail salesman different from both?
    (2) State in what respect they discharge the same functions.
    (3) What line of study should the student follow?

B. QUESTIONS FOR WRITTEN ANSWERS:
    (1) Why is it impossible for one salesman to develop the knowledge and ability to sell *anything?*
    (2) Since every one has something to sell, how many classes of salesmen can you name besides the four mentioned? In what respects does a commercial traveller differ from a doctor.

C

**PRACTICAL LESSONS IN RETAIL
MERCHANDISING**

LESSON THIRTEEN

THE RETAIL SALESMAN—THE RIGHT VIEWPOINT

A SUCCESSFUL Pittsburgh merchant said to me one day, "Any poor, bare-footed, red-headed boy, with the right stuff in him, can walk into this store to-day and eventually force me to make him a partner in the business. Why? Because of the service he can render: he can make himself indispensable."

I have often thought of this remark in connection with an incident that happened in Chicago, which affords a striking contrast. A messenger boy was sent on a special journey to the suburbs, carrying a parcel required in a great hurry. He boarded a surface car and after a time it stopped—something had gone wrong with the mechanism. "How long are we going to be tied up?" asked the boy of the conductor. "Oh not long—where are you going?" The boy told him. "Why that's only two blocks away, why not walk?" said the conductor. "Well I ain't paid to walk," replied the boy as he sank back into his seat. The customer anxiously waiting for the parcel, and perhaps paying for an express delivery, must forsooth wait a little longer because the messenger boy is not "paid for walking."

The lessons of these contrasted incidents are two, and the first is that in the retail store, as elsewhere, the value of one's services is the value that brings success; the second is that retail salesmanship offers as many opportunities as any other calling—perhaps more. The philosophy of this section of the book is one of a great opportunity and how that opportunity may be realized.

I will begin by dealing with the retail store itself. Its real function is to serve the public by supplying its general needs at a fair price. This was not always the idea. The old type of merchant bought goods that he thought he could sell at a considerable profit, and if he found he could not get a high price, he eventually sold at a lower price. He had no primary notion of buying what the people needed, and of thus trying to serve them; his first and only idea was profit. Of course in looking for goods that he could sell he was compelled to think of what people would be likely to buy; but even if he knew they would buy a certain line on which there was a small profit, he would decline it and buy a less needed article that yielded a larger profit.

In these days, however, the merchant acts more in the capacity of a servant of the public, and he finds that it pays. The same principle applies to his salesmen, whose first duty is to get the right viewpoint in relation to their work. In other words, they must find and maintain the right mental attitude towards the customer.

I can illustrate it best in this way. If you had a monopoly for selling carpets, nobody else could deal in them and everybody would come to you to buy. If they grumbled at the price—if you sold a poor quality—if you were uncivil to purchasers—you would not be concerned, for you would know that men and women could buy these things nowhere else. You would be master of the situation and snap your fingers at the criticism which accused you of unfair dealing. You would feel no compulsion to oblige the public, although it might be more pleasant to do so; indeed, you might come to regard yourself as a really kind man who, for a consideration, obliged people with the sale of carpets.

But suppose the government crushed your monopoly and allowed *anybody* to sell carpets—what would be your attitude *then?* Why, you would be eager for business. You would advertise and ask people to inspect your stock. You would be polite when they came, and take good care to serve them well so as to make them come again. If you adopted your old tactics of not caring whether they were satisfied, you would know they could go elsewhere and never return.

The fact of competition makes this difference, and in its beneficent aspects competition is a healthy struggle among traders and merchants, the issue of which is to decide who among them can give the public the most complete and abiding satisfaction.

And herein lies the secret of the salesman's viewpoint. He is a unit in a store, large or small, which has this ideal as a working gospel. The customer is not an enemy to be defeated, or im-

THE ART OF SELLING

prisoned, or robbed; he is a friend with money in his pocket some of which he is ready to part with for a just equivalent in goods. He is not an innocent whose trusting nature is to be exploited for your gain; he is a buyer whom it is your privilege to instruct in the nature and uses of your goods and whose confidence you are to obtain and retain by fair dealing.

There is no profitable selling unless it is mutually beneficial to the customer and the house. Tell a lady a gown is imported when it is not, and it is the same to her in the outcome whether you said it ignorantly or wilfully, for she buys it believing what you have said. The future business of the house suffers in consequence when she finds out that your statement was false.

In retail salesmanship the same laws apply as in every other form of selling. A salesman must know himself, his goods and his customers. And he must know how to apply that knowledge to the end of satisfaction and profit of both buyer and seller. The program is too large to be dealt with in the space at my disposal, so I shall confine my attention to certain points in the practice of selling—its difficulties, its opportunities and its rewards.

EXERCISES

A. QUESTIONS FOR REVIEW:
  (1) What ought a retail man to aim at in order to become comparatively indispensable?
  (2) How does the new idea of a store differ from the old one?
  (3) Describe the true attitude a store salesman should take up with reference to the customer.

B. QUESTIONS FOR WRITTEN ANSWERS:
  (1) Why is it necessary that profitable selling should be mutually beneficial to buyer and seller?
  (2) Show how the retailer is on the same selling platform as other salesmen.

LESSON FOURTEEN

SALESMEN VERSUS ORDER-TAKERS

A RETAIL merchant man was once asked by a friend "How many salesmen have you?" After a moment he replied, "Three." "Why!" exclaimed the friend, "I thought you had quite a force." "Well," he said, "I have a number of persons who stand behind the counter and take orders, but I have only three salesmen—the rest are mere order-takers."

Such men are of little use anywhere. They do not serve their employers and they do not serve the public. Here is an illustration of how the order-taker fails in both respects. A gentleman walked into a drug-store and called for a bottle of patent medicine. An order-taker waited upon him. He looked for the medicine, told the gentleman they had none, and then added, "Nothing else to-day?" The gentleman answered, "No," and with that he turned to go. The proprietor of the store, who was a real salesman, having seen the whole transaction and observing that the gentleman apparently was not in a hurry, spoke to him as follows:

"Pardon me, but are you in a great hurry?" "No sir," answered the gentleman. "Then," replied the proprietor, "just wait a moment and I will have that medicine for you. The wholesale house is only two blocks up—I will have the medicine here in very short order."

By this time he was at the telephone and, calling up the wholesale house, told them to send over a dozen bottles by messenger, and to rush it, as a gentleman was waiting for one. He then turned his attention to his customer, engaged him in pleasant conversation, tactfully attracted his attention to a fine line of gentlemen's toilet articles in the show-case near where they were standing, and by the time the medicine had arrived, or at least before the gentleman had left the store, he had taken an *interest* in some of the things to which the salesman had called *attention,* and his interest changed to *desire,* and his *desire* ripened into *resolve* which was seen in a purchase of $7.00 worth of toilet articles.

The order-taker received $7.50 a week and was rather expensive even at that figure. The proprietor called him, after the customer had departed, and said, "Why did you not do what I have done?" He replied, "I didn't think."

That is the exact truth. If he had only thought a little, he would have sold the medicine and an additional $7.00 worth of goods. This is one great source of difference between a salesman and an order-taker: the latter isn't a thinker. He does not think about the goods, about himself, or about the customer. He is almost an automaton: you pull the string—that is, give an order—and the figure moves—to write the order down or say he does not have the goods. After that, a negative suggestion and—silence.

Now I do not say that, although any man can smile behind a counter and take orders for goods he may happen to possess, therefore any man can easily become an expert salesman. He has much to learn about himself and his education, about the nature and uses of the goods, and the wants of his customers. These three things together form the Science of Business-building* and demand time and study. But I do say that the energy which will redeem a man from being a mere order-taker can be created on the spot by an act of will. Determine to serve your customers well and you will never have to make the humiliating confession "I didn't think," though sometimes you may fail to make a sale.

But there is another kind of order-taker to be dealt with. This time he is engaged in selling mattresses. He was asked by a lady who was accompanied by her husband—an expert salesman himself—for a mattress at a rather moderate price. He exhibited a specimen—waiting for comments or requests from the lady. In other words, he took the order and did nothing else. He knew that, although the displayed mattress was worth the money, it was not such good value as the one a little higher in

---

(*The correspondence course of the Sheldon School in 32 volumes.)

price, but he did not volunteer this information and sell a better article to the increased satisfaction of the purchaser.

Then the lady's husband suggested a mattress of higher quality, and when it was produced the salesman did not attempt to compare and contrast the articles, adducing reasons why the more expensive of the two was preferable. He was destitute of the primary attributes of a salesman's soul and could be classified only as a wooden order-taker.

I hope you will remember this most important distinction:

A salesman really sells things, but an order-taker simply hands you the goods that you mentally bought before you entered the store.

EXERCISES

A. QUESTIONS FOR REVIEW:
  (1) Define an "order-taker."
  (2) Is there any selling art required in the sale of goods which a customer determined to buy before he entered the store? If so, what?
  (3) How would you convert an order-taker into a salesman?

B. QUESTIONS FOR WRITTEN ANSWERS:
  (1) and (2) One or two students should be requested to visit different stores and write a report of their experiences from the standpoint of this lesson.

Reports may be considered at the next lesson, each being read aloud, and the whole class should take part in the discussion.

LESSON FIFTEEN

MENTAL AND MORAL DISCIPLINE

THE first mental power to be developed is that of observation, for although it is through the eye sense we observe things, it is the brain that actually *sees*. And we may see much in this way without gaining any lasting advantage unless the mind interprets what is observed. Hence the observation I speak of is *vision* plus *reflection*—that is, not merely "noticing," but noticing with intelligence. You may see a quantity of quite new goods brought into the store, but if you think no more about the matter, and never trouble to ascertain names, sizes, prices, etc., you are not likely to know much about the new goods.

Detectives are systematically trained in observation by being taken into a room, caused to walk around it once, and then required to write down all they saw and can recall. On the first trial the list contains eight or ten articles fairly well described; but, when trained by repeated trial, they can enumerate sixty to eighty items they saw in that brief time.

Apply the same method to the momentary observations of store windows, and to the display inside. Apply it to persons and see how much information a glance will give you about their faces, eyes, height, walk and other details. The value of this training for the retail salesman lies in its power to supply openings for a sale. You notice this, that and another thing, and use them as a means of introducing your goods, or in otherwise assisting you to effect a sale.

Along with the development of observation should come ear training, and the training of the memory. You may studiously observe life, but if you cannot remember what you see, the studious labor is not of much service.

Here is an illustration of the way in which the eye, the ear and the memory are called upon to work in unison:

There are six people in a department, A, B, C, D, E and F. The buyer said one morning, "Notice this leather bag. There are only a few of the kind left and our repeat order has been delayed in the market. I should like to keep these on display until the others arrive, but try not to sell them. Substitute, if possible, another bag when one of these is called for."

Now, here were instructions to be followed, that were reasonable enough for the skillful salesperson to carry out. Let us see how the six succeeded.

A and B had so trained their ears to hear that they were in the habit of turning their attention at once to the matter in hand. Hence, they heard the first word as well as the last, and their eyes, trained to see, noted the bag. C and D, anxious to show their interest in the buyer, tried to listen, but, not having formed the habits of seeing and hearing accurately, they saw him and understood him, but his words did not make a deep impression. So C forgot which bag he meant and D forgot about the matter entirely until she had one bag partly sold.

E and F, because of inattentive habits, looked around from the end of the counter and thought they heard what he said; but one was fixing her collar and the other was thinking of something else. How many people make practically no use of, or else misuse, their greatest possession and most valuable asset in the money-making world—their brains.

A reflected on instructions and reasoned thus: "If I am to substitute another bag, I must find one that matches this one favorably in good points." She compared several bags with the one in question and picked out one with which she decided to interest customers first, when she saw them attracted to the other bag. This she did.

B went about her work, remembering well her instructions and intending to carry them out; but, when her customer stood in front of her, she was not prepared to act quickly enough to divert her attention.

Which one of all of them showed the most ability? What did A do? She used, first of all, her senses of hearing and sight with effect, because she had trained them well by exercise. Then she concentrated upon the matter and used her reasoning powers well, arriving at a good judgment. She used her imagination in picturing the customer before her and how she would handle her, in order to succeed in following instructions. Lastly, she remembered instructions when the time came to carry them out. Summing up, she exercised her observation, judgment, imagination and memory. And who shall say that each of these powers was not stronger for the exercise given it, and that the mind was not, at the same time, accumulating certain knowledge to be used again?

And who shall say that B, C, D, E and F had the same mental powers to exercise that A did, when they failed to show equal ability in acting upon instructions, thereby falling short of success?

Of the value of memory I can give no more practical illustration than the following which recently appeared in a trade paper:

"If, for instance, a customer shows a decided liking for shades of blue, the wise clerk at the dry goods counter always talks that color, no matter what the fashion of the moment may be. He is sure then to please his customer, both because she gets without effort what she really wants and because she is flattered at having her wants remembered. It is easy enough to do this once; the difficult thing is to remember, the next time that customer appears, to take advantage of what he has already learned about her likes and dislikes. It pleases Mrs. Jones, for instance, to be able to say to the glove clerk, 'I want pale gray; you know the style I wear; send up two pairs.'

"But what if the clerk should forget the name of such a devoted customer? Horrible thought! She probably would not make allowances for the fact that she comes to that counter at comparatively long intervals, and that the clerk has to remember scores and scores of names and the faces that belong to them. She has no difficulty in remembering him, because he is the only clerk from whom she buys silk, or hats, or shoes. All the clerk's tact and skill goes for little, therefore, unless he has a good memory. The mere ability to remember names and peculiarities is valuable. Many a hotel clerk draws a high salary chiefly for the reason that he can call people by name whom he sees only at widely separated intervals. Why is this? Because any one instinctively feels that the man who calls him by name will not 'do' him, or at least that he will not 'do' him so hard. The same principle holds good with the salesman."

The lesson is too obvious to need comment.

The power of speech is still another faculty which calls for training. It is not wholly a mental power, but its main qualities are of the mind, hence a place is found for it in this section. The popular notion is that we do not require tuition in the art of talking—it is something anybody can do—but we seldom go into a store and listen to a selling talk without feeling how much better the salesman might have done had he taken more pains to modulate his voice, to enunciate his words clearly, and to arrange his points skillfully.

Some men and women possess the gift of speech as a natural endowment, but that is no reason why others not so fortunately circumstanced should fail to atone for the want of a natural advantage by careful study and practice. He should learn how to breathe properly so as to avoid "gasping" the last few words of a long sentence; he should learn to be natural and avoid the stilted, artificial style of the man who tries to talk like somebody else; he should dispense with unseemly gestures and tactless remarks by studying good models. Whenever he finds a salesman with a high reputation he may be certain of learning something.

EXERCISES

A. QUESTIONS FOR REVIEW:
  (1) How would you describe the kind of observation necessary to successful retailing?
  (2) What service is rendered by a good memory and a cultivated power of speech?
  (3) Repeat the story of the store clerks A, B, C, D, E, and F.

B. QUESTIONS FOR WRITTEN ANSWERS:
  (1) and (2) The reports of the students (referred to in the last lesson) should now be read and criticised.

LESSON SIXTEEN
DIFFICULTIES

ONE of the worst difficulties a salesperson has to face at the outset is the occasional discourtesy of the customer. A saleswoman tells the following story:

A lady came into the Misses' Coat Department and in a haughty, supercilious tone, said, "I wish to see coats." Knowing that customers frequently get into the wrong coat department, the saleswoman courteously asked, "What kind of coats are you looking for, Madam?" The customer drew herself up and said with acidity, "That is none of your business."

Now the saleswoman, like all energetic people, was inclined to be quick of temper, and for a moment had to battle for her self-control. Then she said in her pleasantest and quietest manner, "Madam, if you wish ladies' coats I would direct you to the right on this floor. If you wish girls' coats, I would direct you to the second floor front. If you wish men's coats you will find them in the first floor annex. Boys' coats are in the department next to the men's. Infants' coats you will please find on the floor above this. But if you wish Misses' coats I shall be very glad to show them to you in this department."

She maintained throughout her talk the same quiet, pleasant tone and courteous manner, but, at the same time, she made it clear to the customer that her original question had been asked for the customer's own benefit. The latter here mumbled that it was girls' coats she wished and went on her way.

There is no denying the fact that this lady was not only foolish but abominably rude, and yet from a business viewpoint, indeed, from any viewpoint, was it not wiser to return a calm and courteous answer than to "give her as good as she gave?" To return impertinence for impertinence is never the sign of a master mind, and the saleswoman who answered the retort "That's none of your business" by a kind and full statement of the facts about coats, made the so-called lady look like a vulgarian. Possibly the saleswoman had to school herself and thus learn the art of patience before she could quell the feelings of anger, but the schooling was a good investment—one which all salespersons should make at the outset of their career.

Another difficulty is *the effort to please the unpleasable*. Some people seem determined to be dissatisfied with everything you say and everything you do. Be calm about it, however; there's a reason, and you will discover it before long. Try your best to please, and if you fail, never mind. You have this consolation, that the probability is your sour customer will very likely return, for not all salesmen will maintain a sweet attitude towards sour people. Here is a story of how one man won:

"A lady stepped from the elevator into our carpet room. She had an unpleasant expression of countenance as she asked in a caustic tone if I could match a piece of carpet which she took from her satchel. It looked faded and worn. I at once felt that something or some one had displeased her. Offering her a chair I said in a reassuring tone that we had several patterns of carpets that would nearly match the sample. I rolled the carpets out so she could look at them and still be comfortable, being anxious that even in so small a purchase she should receive the most thorough attention.

"I then tried to gain her approval of my manner, showing her in a deferential way quite a number of patterns. She gradually grew more agreeable and talkative. Finally, she thanked me for my attention, selected one of the patterns recommended by me and ordered three yards. I then asked her if she wanted any more floor coverings or draperies. She replied in a very pleasant manner, 'Yes I do. I wish a parlor carpet.' And she bought one, the sale amounting to $60.00. By this time she had completely thawed out and explained why she had been so caustic. She had been to several stores and when she had shown her worn sample the salesmen had acted as though they were afraid to touch it, at the same time telling her they had never had goods like it and that she had better try elsewhere."

It will generally be found that the majority of unpleasable folk are amenable to proper treatment; those who are not are of

THE ART OF SELLING

the chronic type—they turn over a score of articles, or sizes, or colors, and are dissatisfied at the end because they really do not know WHAT they want. But accept them with good humor. They appreciate courtesy, although they wouldn't let you think so for the world.

A third difficulty is that of having to deal with two or three customers at once. Very often this is a tribute to your excellence. A lady enters the store and walks to the suit department. "I wish Miss Brisk," she says. "Miss Brisk has a customer. Perhaps you would like Miss C to help you to save time," suggests the floor manager. "No, I'll wait for Miss Brisk." You look and see Miss Brisk waiting upon one customer, with another at her elbow, and this one waiting. Then you hand over a customer to Miss C. Five minutes later the customer leaves, no package in her hand, no money at the desk, and Miss C idle. Another customer comes in, asks for Miss Brisk, and waits for her. The next one coming in you direct to Miss C. In five minutes she leaves—no package, no money—Miss C idle again. The floor manager determines on some radical changes, but Miss Brisk's difficulties arise out of her very excellencies as a saleswoman.

In times of bargain sales every salesperson will be working at high pressure, and occasionally during slacker periods it will be necessary to serve more than one customer at the same time. But the art is not difficult to learn, and if you find the customer has asked for you be rather pleased than annoyed. True it is not pleasant to have a customer tap the counter and draw your attention when you are in the midst of a selling talk to another customer, but a little patience and a smile will carry you through.

EXERCISES

A. QUESTIONS FOR REVIEW:
  (1) Illustrate the difficulty of a salesperson in dealing with a discourteous customer.
  (2) How would you handle the apparently unpleasable person?

(3) Prove that a small crowd of customers may be a difficulty to the salesperson and yet a compliment to his (or her) gifts.

B. QUESTIONS FOR WRITTEN ANSWERS:
(1) What qualities in a salesperson cause the customer to wish to be served again by that salesperson?
(2) Criticise the following dialogue:
Saleswoman—"What can I show you this morning Madam?"
Customer—(Snappishly) "Nothing. Where's Miss Bruce?"
Saleswoman—"Miss Bruce is no longer here."
Customer—"Which means she was too good for the place."
Saleswoman—(Acidly) "Is there not anything I can show you?"
Customer—"Absolutely none." (Goes away.)

LESSON SEVENTEEN
THE HARM OF NEGATIVE SUGGESTIONS

I ONCE went into a haberdasher's store to buy a collar and pair of cuffs. One of the greatest selling forces in the world, necessity, had attracted my attention to the fact that I needed those articles. I had been compelled to take an interest in them for appearance' sake; I had come to desire them and had resolved to buy them. In one sense, therefore, the sale had been made before I entered the store.

A man approached me and I made known my wants. He handed me a package with the change. I found out later he had forgotten to include the collar. This was poor service, due either to forgetfulness or lack of observation—not paying attention to what I said. His mind was probably fixed on something else.

But that was not the only blunder he made. As I turned to go, he said, "You *don't* want any neckties, *do you?*" Of course he did not emphasize it just that way. In fact he did not place any special emphasis anywhere. But that is what he said, although it was not what he meant. And yet it is what we say and do in the great field of life that counts.

Now this man suggested to me that I did not want any neckties. My very natural answer to his suggestion was "No."

There is a humorous side to this particular incident. Within three days after this event occurred, my attention was called to the fact that I *did* need some neckties in spite of the statement of the order-taker that I did not want any.

I went into another haberdasher's store only three doors from the first one, and there I bought three ties, or rather I bought one and the salesman sold me two more. He was not offensively persistent; he did not annoy me in any way. He accomplished what he did, not by suggesting I needed no more ties, but by drawing my attention to the new patterns and good values he was offering for sale. He got my attention, aroused my desire, and secured a decision to buy. I was glad then and am glad now I bought three ties. He served me well.

And this salesman did not stop there. He showed me a five-dollar neckscarf, remarking, "I know you must enjoy looking at good things. You don't seem to be in a hurry this morning, and I want you to see our fine line of neckscarfs." Again he had my attention, my interest and my desire. But for some reason I stopped there. Desire did not ripen into action. Possibly I had not the five dollars with me. But as I was passing the store a few mornings later I saw the neckscarfs beautifully displayed in the window, and the desire to possess one was reawakened and intensified. Whereupon I entered and bought one.

I have traded more or less at this store ever since. I have never been to the other store, three doors away, since the day that the order-taker told me that I did not want the ties I needed —in fact the store is no longer there.

Every story has its moral, and the moral here for the embryo salesman is, "Never offer a customer a negative suggestion." If you are anxious to *sell,* why talk to him in a way that makes him think he has no wants and therefore need not buy? Your object is to make a sale, and instead of saying, "I suppose these are not in your line?" or "You wouldn't care for that?" or "I presume it's no good offering you this?"—all of which are negative suggestions —you take the positive line and begin to describe the virtues of what you have in your store. Don't trouble your mind about his wants. Talk business affirmatively and discover wants, for not every man knows all his immediate needs. I myself, for instance, in the case referred to, was in want of neckties and did not know it. The salesman did not embarrass me through persistency. He merely suggested to me that as the ties were a very fine stock, the sale gave good values; that I would soon need more; and that this would be a good time to lay in a small supply.

But negative suggestions spring out of a negative attitude of mind and are not always embodied in phrases such as "You don't want any neckties, do you?" They are seen in the mere absence of something positive. Here is an illustration:

A lady enters a store to buy a hat, and has to pass the jewelry counter. She is not interested in bracelets at the moment, but a pretty display attracts her attention. A saleswoman steps up and says, "These are $5.00, madam."

A more positive saleswoman might have said, provided the statement was strictly true, "Madam, we've only had those bracelets out half an hour and we've sold three of them already. They are *only* $5.00."

Now, although the first saleswoman did not offer a negative suggestion, what she did say was so coldly affirmative that, compared with the bright and telling remark of the second saleswoman, it is charged with a good deal of negative influence, because it does not say enough and does not say well what it does say.

The lesson is this: In addressing customers about their own needs, or in talking about your goods, always follow the positive line. Say something affirmative. People enter a store to see what is offered for sale, and it is your business to find something that will appeal to them in the line of probable service; not to suggest they don't want anything.

EXERCISES

A. QUESTIONS FOR REVIEW:
  (1) Define "negative suggestion."
  (2) Contrast a negative phrase with a positive phrase and show the advantage of the latter.
  (3) Can a true salesman ever employ the negative suggestion? Give reasons.

B. QUESTIONS FOR WRITTEN ANSWERS:
  (1) Show how the discovery of wants is the salesman's objective.
  (2) Compare negative and positive suggestions as means for persuading the customer to buy.

LESSON EIGHTEEN
POSITIVE SUGGESTION

WHEN a salesman has sold the goods asked for by a customer it is his privilege to draw the customer's attention, tactfully and not aggressively, to other articles. High art in selling is something in advance of order-taking. It must be admitted that certain valuable gifts are exercised in serving the customer along the line of goods he has requested, but in one sense the sale was begun before he entered the store. He had practically determined to buy. A salesman, who has some claims to be an artist in his work, sizes up his customer, and begins to suggest additional purchases by displaying a new and attractive article, although he may never even ask the customer to buy it. He is busy getting attention, creating interest, and arousing desire.

Should the customer become a buyer, the salesman is to be congratulated, for he has not used an unpleasant form of persuasion that compels a purchaser to buy what he does not want—there is no science in that. He who is persuaded to accept goods against his better judgment is not likely to return for more goods; he will be afraid of a salesman who is too pressing.

And yet every customer has needs of which he is glad to be reminded; but the salesman must remind him in the right way at the right time. To speak in a voice which has not the right inflection, or to detain a man who is in a hurry, is not to render service. The salesman must follow instinct and the judgment of experience in deciding such matters as these.

I enter a store to buy shirts, and, having bought them, I turn to leave, when the salesman tactfully mentions "cuff links." I have not the slightest intention of buying anything of the kind. and at first I say "No," but almost immediately I remember that I had decided to buy a better pair than those I am using. So I face the salesman and he, ever alert to read my thoughts as expressed in action, is instantly ready with the article. I feel at the end of his talk that I know what I am buying, and, although I am spending nearly twice as much as I intended to do, I may not have trouble with cuff links for some years to come.

Now the salesman, by suggestion of a positive kind, was bringing to remembrance a decision I had arrived at previously to purchase at some future time a pair of cuff links; and in so doing he was rendering me a service. As it happened, I needed the links sooner than I had imagined, and, as I was satisfied with my purchase, the sale was advantageous on both sides.

It may be urged it was only a chance that the salesman hit upon something I had determined to buy beforehand; he might have said "cuff links" only to find me well supplied. Yes, but in that case, on hearing my "No," it would have been his duty, granted a favorable occasion, to say something else—"Studs," for instance—and begin by actually displaying them. He might say, "Here is a new patent collar stud which has never yet caused an evil word to be spoken by the wearer." I should be inclined to look at it on that account, because evil words are often spoken about collar studs, and my curiosity would be aroused to see the article that maintained the purity and propriety of the English language. By this time the salesman is showing me the mechanism—which is simple but very clever—and as the price is only 25c I feel inclined to buy one notwithstanding I already possess others.

Perhaps I end by buying a pair, but in any case the salesman has not unduly pressed me, and he has not sold me what I do not want. What he did was to use positive suggestion, and if he had not been successful in this instance he might have been in another.

A good deal depends on the way it is done. For instance, in dealing with silk, here is a list of commonplace remarks addressed to a lady purchaser:

This silk has a very pretty design.
It is soft silk.
It is easy to handle and make up.
You will find that the colors in this silk match one another well.

Here is a better list—with *suggestive powers:*
This silk shimmers.
It has a soft lustre.

It falls readily in graceful folds.
It clings to the figure.
The design merges into the background and does not startle the eye.
The colors blend with an exquisite harmony.

The chief difference between these two lists is that each point in the first is so elementary that the customer can see it for herself, but in the second each point is so stated that it carries with it some suggestion that might not otherwise come into the mind of the customer. For a salesman to say a thing is pretty or beautiful is no convincing argument—it is merely a statement of his individual taste; but, if he can show reasons why it is beautiful, and direct the customer by suggestive statements to see its beauty, then he is leading the purchaser to desire and to resolve.

EXERCISES

A. QUESTIONS FOR REVIEW:
  (1) Can a salesman unduly press a customer to buy? Show how.
  (2) What is the difference between this undue pressure and questions directed to the discovery of the customer's needs?
  (3) Illustrate a positive suggestion so poor in positive power as to be almost equivalent to a negative.

B. QUESTIONS FOR WRITTEN ANSWERS:
  (1) and (2) Why is the commonplace remark, "Anything else today?" useless as a suggestion?

  Note: One or two students should be asked to visit different stores for small purchases and to note the number and quality of positive suggestions made to them by the salesmen. Reports of these visits should be given to the class at the next lesson.

LESSON NINETEEN
ANALYZE YOUR GOODS

THE reasons that lead a store proprietor to buy goods to sell again are the reasons that will lead the purchaser to buy them. Consequently every article in the department of which you are a salesman has a reason for its presence in the store; and it is your duty to know what that reason is and to be able to enforce it. To do this requires an analysis. Take a piece of dress goods. You analyze it as follows:

1. Is it imported or domestic?
2. What is its design—color—texture?
3. What is its utility—value—width—price?

No. 1 is easily answered. No. 2 may result in the following answers: It is new this season—it is an advance idea—it is an exclusive make—it is adapted to a mature woman—not for a miss or a girl—not suitable for a stout person, etc.

Take design in relation to the next point—color. How does the color harmonize with the design? What color is in the background, what in the foreground? How different from old designs?

Then take design in relation to texture—woven the same on both sides: in relation to utility—not strong, as it is a fad design; conspicuous and not made for staple wear: in relation to price—novelty makes it high.

Design in relation to the whole: suitable for tailored garments with little trimming, etc.

Take every other point and study it in the same way.

The object of such an analysis is to enable you to talk intelligently about the things you handle, and to improve your chances of selling them. The examples given are intended as illustrations of general principles; they can be applied to every class of goods.

A very successful salesman of men's neckwear was asked what points he studied about his goods. He said:

"Get a general idea of what your customer wants. Know the

shapes, lengths, widths, weights; the silks that are the most desirable for rough wear; the season's latest fads as to coloring, shapes, fabrics; what is the most suitable for church, theatre, receptions, weddings; for morning, noon, or night; for outing or business purposes; how the necktie is made, and why cut a particular shape, or this or that width. Learn to tie all shapes quickly and correctly for exacting trade. Make it a pleasure to give minute instruction as to tying different knots. In other words, to be successful, know what you are talking about, and don't talk too much."

Now this man may be called a scholarly salesman. There is no point on the grammar, composition, and uses of neckties with which he is unfamiliar. That is one of the reasons why he is so successful. If he were asked "Who made the first necktie?" possibly he could tell you, for he has taken a deep interest in his line, not only in its present conditions but in its past history.

You may say he is an unusual salesman. Not at all. You can meet men who talk about carpets and cook stoves in just the same intelligent way. They are commercial scholars, and every salesman should aim at this kind of accomplishment. It means greater service to the customer, and greater service spells more profit to the proprietor, as well as more remuneration to the salesman.

I do not deny that to get such a knowledge of your goods takes time, but it is worth the trouble. Cut out a few hours from the pastimes and recreations that swallow dollars instead of making them, and devote those hours to analyses. You will find the work interesting in itself, and you know all the time it has a side to it that means promotion; whilst the added pleasure and zest it gives to the art of selling amply compensates the loss of an occasional game of billiards or a seat at the theatre.

EXERCISES

A. QUESTIONS FOR REVIEW:
    (1) What is the reason for an analysis of the goods?
    (2) How would an analysis be worked out in relation to a piece of dress goods?

(3) Go over the ground covered by the description of a neckwear salesman.

B. QUESTIONS FOR WRITTEN ANSWERS:

(1) and (2) Reports on the students' visits to stores (referred to in the previous lesson) should be discussed.

LESSON TWENTY
A Specimen Selling Talk

THE retail salesman can, as a rule, plunge into his selling talk without any preliminaries, because the customer's wants are stated at once. It sometimes happens, however, that the customer is not at all clear as to what his wants are, and he needs approaching with a sort of preliminary talk, the object of which is to assist him in defining the object he wishes to purchase. Here, for instance, is an illustration of what I mean. It is from the note-book of an experienced salesman:

"Some few days ago I noticed a lady slowly approaching my section, who, from her appearance, I imagined to be a stranger amusing herself by comparing the prices of our goods with those of the little suburban stores where she usually purchased her wares. Not one characteristic of the shopping woman did she display.

"I watched her as she slowly approached my section, seemingly taking in everything and silently enjoying herself, until near enough to address her—without that swift business air which seems to say, 'If there is nothing you wish, please keep moving,'—but very courteously, and in the same spirit as was manifested by her, said, 'Madam, is there anything you wish?' She stopped, hesitated, looked doubtful, and I said, 'Or can I be of service to you?' —which seemed to touch a chord of harmony within her; for she smiled and said, 'Why yes, but I scarcely think you can supply what I want, or even direct me where to find it, as I have been, it seems, in every department of this big store and have not yet found what I want.' 'Well that seems strange; I always supposed this store kept for sale almost everything but fresh fish and rib roast.'

"She laughed and said, 'I presume they do, but before you direct me where to go you must first tell me what I want as I myself do not know.' And then she told me she was trying to find something to purchase as a present for a friend who was very dear to her, and who in a few days expected to celebrate her sec-

THE ART OF SELLING

ond wedding anniversary. 'But of course,' she added, 'you have nothing down here which would be appropriate for such a gift, and I fear you could scarcely direct me where to find it.' 'Madam,' I replied, 'if you will allow me a few moments of your time—,(kindly step this way,' leading her to the bamboo utility boxes), 'I think I can show you something that will not only make a very pretty and appropriate gift to such a friend but one that is practical, one that she will use every day and enjoy as much as anything you could give her.'"

The rest of the story is not material to the purpose of this chapter. Let it suffice to say that a sale for sixteen dollars was made and the lady departed quite satisfied with her purchase.

To get up a selling talk about your goods is one thing; to take the initiative and assist a purchaser in finding out her own needs is another thing. The first is like a prepared speech which can be addressed to almost any audience; the second is a form of approaching the customer that calls for tact and initiative. And yet it is a selling talk because it is a preliminary that leads up to a sale; it is the adjustment between the undefined needs of the purchaser and the goods you have to sell. Be ready then to preface your main list of reasons for a purchase by a little diplomatic handling of the customer who may not know exactly what he intends to purchase.

Order-filling takes up a large part of every salesman's day: he carries out the wishes of a customer, wraps up the goods and collects the money. In these sales some knowledge and art are called into requisition—although a sale was made before the customer came into the store. But when an order has been filled there comes the salesman's real opportunity. Having sold some collars, he can now display some ties. He has some at hand, of new and exclusive design, on which the profits are larger than on the ordinary run of goods. He must first of all get attention with his *introduction*. "Have you seen these new maple-leaf ties? It's a new design, and exclusive as yet. These came in this morning and are the only ones on the market here."

Or

"Have you ever noticed how a man's tie gives character to

his whole appearance? A poorly chosen tie can spoil everything, even if the rest of the outfit is in good taste; while a neat, modish and well-set cravat gives distinction, even if the rest of the clothing is a little below par. With the rest of the apparel in keeping, a good tie gives a man the feeling of power that comes with the knowledge of being well dressed—but not over-dressed. Now here is the new maple-leaf tie. It will illustrate what I mean."

There are any number of good introductions that can be used. As has been said so often before, each must fit the occasion. Having gained the customer's attention by means of the introduction, the next thing is to arouse his interest, awaken his desire, and bring about his action with the first selling talk.

FIRST SELLING TALK:

"These ties are made by the Walden Co., whose trade-mark is a sign of quality. Just feel the material. Notice how rich and soft the silk is. That keeps the tie from wrinkling, so that it looks fresh and neat much longer than the ordinary tie. Then this shape is a special design to go with the new styles in collars that are so popular just now. You see this one I have on—how well it sits. Notice the colors, too—all beautiful but quiet and harmonious shades. The patterns of the silk are new and exclusive, too. These were all designed and woven expressly for the Walden Co. in Lyons, France. Don't you think that is a very pretty pattern?"

Usually, by this time, the customer has indicated in some way which colors and patterns he prefers. He looks longer at the ties that please his fancy or gets them together in one little heap. Or he asks a question or two about them. Nearly always he gives the alert salesman a little peep into his mind. Some salesmen then find it best to put away all but the goods the customer seems to favor. This will depend upon circumstances, but it is a good rule not to distract the customer's attention and confuse his judgment by presenting too many articles or kinds of articles at one time.

Watch for the psychological moment. When it arrives, close, no matter where you are in your selling talk. You are not talking for the sake of hearing yourself talk, or because you have been paid to say a certain thing—no more and no less—you are talking to sell goods. When the goods are sold, stop talking and take the order.

The close may be in words, asking some question as to how many, which patterns, what sizes, delivery, charge or cash, or the customer's name and address. Or it may be by a gesture, as by gathering up the articles and reaching for the wrapping paper, taking out pencil and sales-book, or some other preparatory movement. These things soon become habitual with the salesman. But they should be constantly studied for flaws, and assiduously improved. A good habit is a great asset, but a rut is a grave.

SECONDARY SELLING TALK:

But suppose the psychological moment is not reached. Desire is not yet strong enough. You must appeal to your customer's imagination in some way. It will depend upon his temperament. Suppose he is a keen, practical business man, neatly and quietly dressed in clothing of excellent quality. Your secondary selling talk would be along these lines:

"You can tell by the feeling of these ties that they are of heavy, extra quality material. There is a satisfaction in possessing and wearing an article that has so much character. Then they are stylish and handsome without being conspicuous. There is a desirable middle ground not always easy to find. Will you have them charged?" But suppose you were to meet with an objection—that the price was too high, the colors not becoming, or the goods too heavy? If you know that these ties would serve your customer, each of these objections, and any others, can be tactfully overcome.

EXERCISES

A. QUESTIONS FOR REVIEW:
  (1) What is the "preliminary" talk?
  (2) Does it differ in any way from the *introduction* referred to? How?
  (3) What is the object of the first selling talk?
B. QUESTIONS FOR WRITTEN ANSWERS:
  (1) What is the object of the introduction?
  (2) How does this lesson use the mental law of sale?

LESSON TWENTY-ONE
ANSWERING OBJECTIONS

WHEN you have offered an article to a customer and he says, disparagingly, "I can get it much cheaper at Frank's" what are you going to say by way of reply? Even if you know he is not telling the truth, it would never do to say, "You *can't* buy it cheaper at Frank's," for that would be equivalent to saying he is a liar. Perhaps he honestly thinks he can go to Frank's and buy the thing at fifty cents less than you are asking for it, and he has come to that conclusion because he cannot distinguish qualities as well as you can.

Your reply therefore must be one which enlightens him on the difference between appearance and reality. Frank's goods may *appear* to be like yours but possibly are *not* because of certain points which you proceed to exhibit to your customer. But dispense this information tactfully and allow that the external appearance is so close as to justify the notion of identity in quality. In popular parlance, "let him down easily."

Of course it sometimes happens that the customer is in the right: he *can* buy cheaper elsewhere and you are not aware of the fact. Don't throw out a challenge offering $5.00 if he can buy the same article at Frank's store at the same price. He may take you at your word and bring an identical article with a bill charging fifty cents less than you do, because the Frank's manager is selling at cost price as an advertisement. You would look foolish in those circumstances, and the best way to prevent so awkward a happening is to allow the customer his opinion and let him go. To argue with him only irritates him, even if he be deceived; and when he is right it maddens him. An attitude of polite interest towards the prices of your competitor is advisable, but it seldom pays to debate them with customers, especially to cast aspersions on the honesty of other firms' figures. A positive assurance of fair value and the rendering of good service is the best salesmanship.

Another objection often met with is: *I can't spare the money.* On the face of it the objection is sensible, for if a man says he cannot spare the money, it is either a polite way of saying he has no money at all or else that he really needs what he has for something else. But, having granted this, it must be admitted that the objection is frequently unintelligent and that the customer *can* spare the money only he does not know it. It is your duty and pleasure to inform him. Typewriters are really specialty articles, but as they are stocked by many retailers you may have been trying to sell him one; and, failing to convince him on the usual lines, you ask him, in view of his objections, whether there is any other form of expenditure which would be so calculated to increase his gross receipts. Tell him that money put into office correspondence, insuring an attractive and businesslike appearance, is money which *ought* to be spent because it is well invested and tends to bring in more money. Handwritten letters, especially the half-legible variety, only drive business away. Therefore the plea that the money cannot be spared is one which reveals the objector as standing in his own light—indeed, it is a version of being "penny wise and pound foolish."

Akin to this objection of not being able to spare the money to buy is the one which says, "I can't afford it." Here again we say the objection may be quite true and calls for due attention on that basis. But there is another side. "Can you afford to do *without* the article offered you? What will it cost you to be minus the goods? Mr. Smith of Broughton, whom you know, once argued as you do but he came to the conclusion that he could no longer put off a purchase which meant more efficiency in his office work as well as a larger income. He even put off purchases of other articles when he saw the business bringing power of this one, and we think you will do the same."

These are specimens of the objections the retail salesman will meet in the course of his daily duties, and there are one or two rules he should observe in order to meet them effectively.

(1) Never argue the customer's opinions. Meet his objections by additional reasons for purchase. His opinions about his own needs may be wrong, but they are his opinions all the

same, and the best way to refute them is to argue from the basis of a desirable purchase rather than from the rightness or wrongness of his opinions.

(2) Never lose your temper. A customer may snap out an objection, but let your answer be accompanied by a smile—a real one, not a smirk which he may regard as disdain. You have everything to gain by being cheerful.

(3) Remember the principle that it is not true service to load a customer with anything that he does not want. You may try to convince him he *needs* it, but he may have many commercial needs he cannot afford to pay for, and this may be one. A selling talk should never be so pressing as to compel the buyer to buy against his better judgment. It puts him on his guard against you and you are not likely to succeed again. It is impossible for a salesman to know all the details of a customer's financial responsibilities; and after urging the claims of the goods he can safely do no more. After that it were better to leave the matter for a later occasion.

EXERCISES

A. QUESTIONS FOR REVIEW:
   (1) How would you deal with an objection you knew to be false, and one about which you are not certain?
   (2) Is the plea of not being able to spare the money one that can be met intelligently? If so, how?
   (3) What rules are useful as guides in answering objections?

B. QUESTIONS FOR WRITTEN ANSWERS:
   (1) Analyze the objection "I can't afford it."
   (2) How would you deal with a customer who objected to your proposal that he should buy by saying, "My experience is this stuff does not wear well?"

D
WHOLESALE SELLING

LESSON TWENTY-TWO
Preparing for a Journey

WHEN a salesman contemplates a selling tour he has to make certain preparations for the duties involved; and these duties concern his own selling powers, his goods, the customer, and the organization of the journey.

If he be a comparatively new traveller the amount of self-preparation will be considerable; and even an experienced man feels the need of constant attention to the intensifying of the "story" he is to tell to the customers. A selling talk cannot be constructed as if it were an oration, intended more as an exhibition of eloquence than anything else; it has to *do* something, namely, sell goods, and this calls for a way of putting things that demands an analysis of the goods in relation to the customers, as well as a study of the arts of speech.

I don't exaggerate in the least when I say that the best salesmanship requires as advanced an education, in the professional sense, as good accountancy or good legal practice. The realization of this fact is one reason why the subject is finding its right place in the college curriculum.

The knowledge of men, demanded by the work of wholesale canvassing, is not alone the ability to judge character from external signs, but an acquaintance with a customer's standing in the community, and with his financial condition. As far as possible these items are gathered together by the salesman before he goes out on the journey, often furnished by his firm to be supplemented if needs be by further inquiries on the spot. The object of all this preparation is to avoid weaklings, men who will order goods in large quantities for which they cannot pay; and many items bearing on a man's relatives, his politics, social life, or religion, may have a direct bearing on his character as a trustworthy person and desirable patron. The hotel clerk or the local banker may be sought out and "sounded" for the needed details, or such of them as the salesman has not already in his possession.

Further, he must draw a map of his journeys, so as to waste

no time or money in doubling back on his tracks. If he be travelling from New York to Chicago, by Buffalo, and at Cleveland finds he must return to a city half way to Buffalo, he is spending the firm's money badly and wasting his own time. Hence every good salesman organizes his journey on strictly topographical lines —every place he has to visit is down on the map, and he cleans up one before he goes on to another—there is no turning back to a forgotten city.

When you meet a wholesale salesman, or commercial traveler as he is usually designated, at the railroad depot just about to start on a long trip, you cannot see the amount of preparation that has preceded the journey. He has spent long hours in cultivating the selling talk, in finding out the arguments for purchase, in arranging them, and in phrasing them. He has amassed details about the customers he will interview, and his pocket case often contains a little private biography of every one of them—to be made more detailed after inquiries on the ground. The improvements in his goods are summarized, compared, contrasted, and argued, and he carries a map on which he and his directors may have spent several weeks in discussion before the red lines of the route were finally decided upon. Thus to see the salesman at work does not suggest any special preparation, but as a matter of fact, every man who is really well equipped to sell has gone through some programme very similar to the one outlined in this lesson.

EXERCISES

A. REVIEW QUESTIONS:
  (1) What are the four subjects to which a wholesale salesman gives special attention in preparing for a journey?
  (2) How does he ascertain the standing of the customer?
  (3) Why is it important to have a carefully drawn map of the journey?

B. QUESTIONS FOR WRITTEN ANSWERS:
  (1) Give reasons for the desirability of possessing sound information as to a customer's financial standing.
  (2) "It is easy to be a wholesaleman. All you have to do is to carry your samples, show them, write down the order and send it off by post." Criticise this statement.

LESSON TWENTY-THREE
Technical Knowledge of the Goods

IN wholesaling it is generally agreed that a high standard of knowledge is necessary to insure a salesman's success. A brilliant man may, at times, have done well in selling articles so different as groceries, clothing, and hardware, and he may boast of an ability to sell anything you care to give him; but the chances are if he had stuck to one thing he would have done better than by moving about with a variety.

A sales manager has said: "I would rather have a man in my sales force who was a poor salesman and a good hardware man than the most gifted salesman who had no knowledge, or only a superficial knowledge, of the hardware business. Perhaps the poor salesman would hardly more than pay his expenses at the start, but he would at least avoid making costly mistakes. The gifted salesman, on the other hand, without a knowledge of the hardware business, might send in a tremendous quantity of orders; but the profits would probably be all eaten up when his blunders had been rectified and his disgruntled customers appeased."[*]

To be a wholesale salesman, therefore, means, (among other qualifications), an extensive and accurate acquaintance with the goods; and to give some idea of what such a range of knowledge includes, I will quote from another sales manager:

"In selling varnish, he should know that a varnish is made up of gums, dryers, oils, turps, etc.; he should be familiar with the different gums, both hard and soft; and he should know what class of varnish is suitable for inside or outside work, and what the essential difference is. He should also be familiar with their working qualities: how freely they flow; if they will stand rubbing and polishing; how they dry; how long they should be given before sanding; and he should grasp the distinction between liquid dryers, japans, and such like, for house paints, enamels, and varnish stains, carriage paints and kindred goods known to the trade as paint spe-

---
[*] 125 Brain Power Business Manual, pp. 69-70.

cialties. He would be the better knowing the various pigments contained in his goods; how and where they are produced; what their characteristics are; why some are non-dryers and vice versa; what their requirements are in the way of vehicles and thinness, and whether fast to light or not; why certain combinations are admissible or advisable, and others dangerous or detrimental."

This catalogue of details, by no means full, will give the student an idea of the amount of information, theoretical and practical, which a wholesale salesman is expected to have in readiness for immediate use. It is not knowledge for display but knowledge for service—that of persuading a customer to buy. With it he may succeed; without it he may fail. And what is true of varnish is true of every other kind of goods—technical requirements are demanded of every efficient traveller.

For this reason it is urged that a man should grow up with his line and know it by second nature. There are doubtless certain advantages in learning the art of selling by going out with different classes of goods, but modern practice is tending more and more in the direction of special training for special work. I know a large hardware firm in the West which has taken on only one man from the outside in the space of five years. The policy followed is to start a youth in the basement, raising him step by step until he is prepared by knowledge and experience to become a traveller. Even the Sales Manager is a man who used to be on the road for this house; consequently he knows outside conditions as well as the travellers themselves.

If therefore the representing of a wholesale house is your ambition, be ready to begin at the bottom and grow up in the atmosphere of the goods you are to sell some time in the future. It is a mistake to seize a few samples, hastily study them, and then sally forth to sell. Rather learn how to sell your services to a good firm, then acquire an intimate acquaintance with the goods from the inside. After that you may hope to be a salesman of quality, as distinct from the man whose real description is a hawker of samples.

EXERCISES

A. QUESTIONS FOR REVIEW:
  (1) Enumerate the advantages of knowing the technical qualities of the goods.
  (2) Illustrate these advantages by referring to varnish.
  (3) What is the benefit of "growing up" with a special line of goods?

B. QUESTIONS FOR WRITTEN ANSWERS:
  (1) Imagine you are selling shoes; draw up a brief list of questions which might be asked about their composition and manufacture.
  (2) Compare the advantages of (a) growing up with one line of goods, and (b) of getting experience by first going round with a variety.

LESSON TWENTY-FOUR
GETTING AN INTERVIEW

THE obtaining of an interview is, as may be imagined, a primary matter to every salesman. It is often supremely difficult for the specialty man; and sometimes it is equally so for the wholesale traveller. But the latter has one advantage: in time he becomes known and his orders are given regularly, consequently he has not the maneuvering to do that once fell to his lot in order to obtain a hearing. And yet, if he is progressive, he is always breaking new ground, adding new customers, and in doing this he must use all the arts of interview-getting.

The great barrier everywhere is the subordinate who guards the seclusion of the principal or of the principal's buyer. Salesmen do not decrease in numbers, and this fact causes the merchant to hedge himself round with all sorts of protective devices. He is "not at home" to salesmen on certain days, and if you chance to hit upon one of those days you are fighting "a stiff proposition" to get an interview. In fact, it is wisest not to fight at all, but write him a courteous note, regretting he is too busy to see you to-day, but asking him to make an appointment another day, or possibly on your next trip. Whether he does or not, keep calling, but don't waste time waiting. I have known a salesman wait for two hours to see a merchant and then not see him. This is not salesmanship; it is an unholy sacrifice of opportunity. If you cannot see one man, see another. Unless you can get an interview how can you hope to sell your goods? If you cannot see him on your present trip, call on your next trip and keep on calling. Some of the best commercial travellers have been known to call upon an obstinate buyer on each visit to his town, for many years, before success finally crowned their efforts.

Opinions vary as to how the private secretary, the chief clerk, or the manager should be treated when they bar the way to the principal's office. The only rule I know is that "circumstances decide cases." When a principal has actually secluded himself for four hours with a foreign deputation you can do no good by offending the subordinate, telling him you know very well Mr. Blank *will* see you if he is shown your card. There are occasions when a merchant is honestly too busy to see anybody, and a man of sense will remember this possibility. On the other hand, you need not meekly acquiesce in the old plea that Mr. Blank is "engaged." You are there to get an interview if you can, and it is a fine opportunity to display your diplomatic gifts in handling the member of the staff so as to arrive at the real truth and use it for your own ends.

I know one salesman who thus learned the secret of a side door entrance by which the principal left for home, and he used his knowledge with good effect; for when the big man opened the door the salesman was waiting for him with a smile and—a taxicab. There was an angry look for a moment, then a short laugh as the merchant, quoting Scripture, said, "Hast thou found me, oh mine enemy?" But the salesman only smiled the more as he opened the door of the taxi and beckoned the other man to enter. The selling talk commenced before the wheels began to go round.

You must be a man of *resource* to win interviews from unwilling people. Too many salesmen become mildly quarrelsome, and after being repeatedly put off they indulge in arguments about having "earned the right to an interview." Never argue about rights. Prove you have them by getting the interview. Argue with yourself, not with the customer.

A young salesman says, "When I approach a big building, alive with the signs and sounds of industry, I feel a sort of *fear*—I am so small and the place is so large—I am only one and there are hundreds before me." True, but why fear anything? You are a man, not a chicken: you have good goods: you represent a good house: the throb and hum of busy-ness is just what you ought to welcome, for you could not sell goods to a dead show. This huge concern wants to make more money and you have something to sell which the management can buy and sell again at a profit. So mount the steps, take the elevator to the offices, and ask confidently for an interview. You are there to bring good news about soap, or cocoa, or pickles, or gum arabic, or whatever product you represent. You are there to render a *real service*. You are there to enable your prospective purchaser to make a good profit on that which he buys from you. He will be glad to see you. Be dominated by the true spirit of service. Work in *that* spirit and interviews you did not get before you will begin to get as a matter of course.

EXERCISES

A. QUESTIONS FOR REVIEW:
   (1) Has the wholesale man a better chance of obtaining interviews than the specialty man? If so, in what way?
   (2) How would you deal with the office staff who try to keep you away from the principal?
   (3) Give reasons why you should ask for an interview with confidence.

B. QUESTIONS FOR WRITTEN ANSWERS:
   (1) Why is it bad salesmanship to wait for a long time in the hope of seeing a customer?
   (2) Read the following dialogue and say who was in the wrong.
   Salesman.—"Is Mr. Jenkins in?"
   Office Man.—"No, he won't be back for an hour."
   Salesman. (Who has just seen Mr. Jenkins come in)—"Pardon me, Mr. Jenkins has just come in. I saw him enter a moment ago."
   Office Man. (Testily)—"You're mistaken. He's on his way here in a friend's automobile." (Turns away.)
   Salesman. (Getting angry)—"I'm *not* mistaken. Please take my card in to him . . . I know Mr. Jenkins when I see him."
   The office man ignores the request, and the salesman begins to say what he thinks of him. In the midst of it all Mr. Jenkins opens his office door and hears some strong language from both disputants.

LESSON TWENTY-FIVE
The Tactics of Selling

THE wholesale salesman has to deal with customers who are business men themselves, alert, acute, and keen on driving a bargain. This fact makes the work of preparation, and the work of actual selling, a strenuous matter; and, possibly, of all selling men, the wholesale man is called upon to think more quickly and act more decisively on the moment than any other. He has much that can be learned from the study of his goods and of men, but he has much that can be learned only from practical experience.

The buyer for a store will naturally try to get good stuff at the lowest possible prices, and when he discusses terms with a salesman it is a battle of wits, the victory going to the man who knows the more and can use his superior knowledge with adroitness and courage.

The buyer, let us suppose, is prepared to buy six products from the salesman, and the prices have been agreed upon for five of these products. They are now debating the sixth. "What price did you say was your lowest?" asks the buyer.

"Twelve cents," replies the salesman.

"I can buy it elsewhere at 11½ cents," rejoins the buyer.

"Twelve cents is the market price and is the best I can do," urges the salesman.

"That being so, please cancel the orders for the other goods. Unless you can sell me this stuff at 11½ I can't buy anything else," concludes the buyer.

The salesman finds himself in a very awkward position. To lose a big order because of a difference of half a cent seems absurd and yet in large consignments it makes a difference. Moreover, a bad precedent is established. If the salesman takes his stand, as he ought to, and refuses to quote below the market price, he will probably find the buyer veering round. Threats to cancel orders already given are not a sign that the goods can be obtained easily elsewhere at the same or lower prices; they are signs that the buyer is "squeezing" the salesman and intends to get a close bargain for his firm. Should the salesman yield he is doomed to be regarded as an easy prey on future occasions, and finds his selling doubly difficult in consequence.

This is but one illustration of what the wholesale man may expect to meet every day of his life. He needs to get rid of self-consciousness, in the sense that he is asking and answering questions like these:

"Am I making a good impression?"
"Am I succeeding?"
"Have I taken a false step?"
"What will he say next?"

All through, from beginning to end, the salesman must be a tactician, arranging beforehand his plan of campaign, leaving nothing to chance; and yet in the battle he must think of nothing else but the victory. This is a point worth illustrating further. Take the method of approaching the customer. He can think out the right words to use and do himself a great service. He discovers three modes of address: bad, indifferent, and good. They are:

Bad—"You don't want any oil, I suppose?"
Indifferent—"Do you want any oil to-day?"
Good—"Are your supplies of oil getting low?"

The bad is bad because it is a negative suggestion; the indifferent is indifferent because it offers too easy an opening to say No; the good is good because frequently the state of supplies is not always known, and to suggest a low state, suggests, in turn, the immediate desirability of remedying it by ordering a new supply.

In this way a study of the tactics of selling is invaluable, but the salesman cannot cover every objection that may be urged, at least not for some time, nor can he provide against every conceivable argument against his prices. As Burns says, "the best laid schemes o' mice and men gang aft agley," and the salesman has to be prepared to do a lot of quick thinking in the course of his day's work. It is at these times that he must unconsciously and instantly use the lessons of study and experience in winning a victory for himself and his firm. Bacon says, "Conference makes a ready man." The salesman knows the fatal pause—that lack of readiness which appears to indicate weakness although it may mean only careful reflection—and he soon learns to avoid it.

EXERCISES

A. QUESTIONS FOR REVIEW:
   (1) What fact, with regard to his customer, makes a wholesale man's difficulties more than usually difficult in actual selling?
   (2) State the three modes of approaching a customer.
   (3) Why should the salesman be a "ready" man in speech?

B. QUESTIONS FOR WRITTEN ANSWERS:
   (1) Show how self-consciousness is a hindrance to good selling.
   (2) Analyze the following argument and say what, in your opinion, is the course the salesman ought to have taken:

   Salesman.—"I am not allowed by my house to take less than $1.00 per pair."

   Merchant.—"I can get them at 95 cents from other houses. Give me your stuff at that price and I will increase my orders for the other goods. If you can't, I shall have to deal elsewhere."

   Salesman.—"But. . . ."

   Merchant.—"Nothing doing. *My* terms or no business."

   Salesman.—"Oh, very well."

LESSON TWENTY-SIX
THE SALESMAN'S "NEWS"

I HEAR that a new man is going to open an up-to-date drugstore in 20th Street. The fittings are to cost $2,000. No end of a swell proposition." If you hear a remark like that from your neighbor in the street-car, and druggists are men on whom you call, you do not need to be told what to do. You make it your business to locate that new store; you get to know all you can about the man; you find time to talk to him about your goods, and you get an order if possible.

Unexpected deals of this kind are bright spots in a salesman's life, and they tend to develop what the journalist calls "a good nose for news." He reads his papers with keen eyes for items that will lead to business openings; he talks to people everywhere with the same object in view; and at last becomes a man with trained senses and a gift for drawing accurate conclusions.

Such inquiries can be pursued without in the least militating against the prescribed duties of a prepared journey. I will suppose you have finished your day's work. After dinner you sit down to read. On the table are the trade papers—not only the two or three dealing with your own line, but with many other lines, some of them related to the one you represent. I advise you to select a few of the most important and read them *carefully*. The news items under the head of "personal mention" may contain something of interest. On the surface the fact that Mr. John S. Winter has gone to Europe, or that Mr. Stephen S. Weston is buying lots in a city near by, may carry no meaning; but if on inquiry Mr. Winter's journey and Mr. Weston's purchases turn out to be serious business undertakings, then, since they are the heads of competing firms, you may get hold of news items that are of great advantage to your own house.

Just as a newspaper aims to be first in publishing a big event, so the wide awake salesman is anxious to take the lead in discovering a new "prospect," or in noting the moves of other firms or the men who represent them. He is a diligent student of persons and events as they come across his path—of journals which record the doings of people whom he does not meet, or events in which he does not participate. The press clippings of business news arranged for by the sales manager are all right in this way; they come from many quarters of the country and are put to good use, but they cannot take the place of individual observation and study on the spot. Nevertheless, a wise salesman will always make the editor and reporter his friends wherever he may be. They are men who "know," and as such are invaluable sources of serviceable information. So far as they can, they are usually willing to talk about the developments in their cities, because they are interested in fostering them; and although sometimes their lips are closed by promises of silence, there are many instances where facts of real worth are freely placed at the disposal of an inquirer.

The local Board of Trade is another source to keep in touch with. It represents the progressive spirit of the community; it stands for new enterprises and is directly concerned with the furtherance of them.

For the rest the salesman is left to his own devices in the finding of new customers: it is a question of keeping his eyes and ears open and of using his brains. There is an old saying that all men are worth about a dollar and a half from their feet to their chin, but for the rest of the way, from the chin upwards, their value ranges from two cents to a million dollars. It may be difficult to reach the latter standard of worth in nosing out new buyers, but it is easy to begin with the other and make your value grow each day.

EXERCISES

A. QUESTIONS FOR REVIEW:
    (1) How is a news item of possible service to a salesman?
    (2) What are the chief sources of a salesman's news?
    (3) Which of the five senses are most used in this connection?

B. QUESTIONS FOR WRITTEN ANSWERS:
    (1) If you were travelling for a firm that manufactured

house furniture, what papers would you read in addition to the one that dealt with furniture? (Ask yourself about the materials used in such a factory and how many kinds of buildings need house furniture.)

(2) What would you do if, as a traveller for a furniture house, you read this item in the local paper: "Rumor has it that we are to have a golf club house and a small hotel at Resinworth?"

LESSON TWENTY-SEVEN
ALMOST PERSUADED

ONE of the irritations of a salesman's life is the failure to convince the customer *fully*. To be successful in part and not altogether is as disappointing as anything well can be. The work of securing favorable attention, creating interest, and arousing desire goes for nothing unless the customer takes action and signs the order form. There must be a reason why he is *almost* but not *fully* persuaded, and it is your duty to discover what that reason is and meet it.

Perhaps it arises out of the customer's native sense of caution—the habit of delaying the announcement of a decision, although it has been mentally recorded already. To deal with idiosyncrasies of this kind demands tact which can only come by experience. It is fatal to press the order form in such circumstances, but the real difficulty is to decide when such circumstances exist. How are you to know that the customer has inwardly decided on a purchase but refuses to commit himself outwardly? By trying him with all your closing arguments, or as many of them as are adaptable to his case. If he dodges every one you may conclude he has some private reason for refusing his name on the dotted line.

The probability, however, is that he fails to act because in some manner you have failed to *convince* him. As a rule the man who is thoroughly convinced admits the fact and proves it by offering his signature. Hence the almost persuaded customer should be discreetly questioned until you have covered most of the arguments in commission and discovered the cause of his hesitation. This calls for much skill, otherwise you will quite unintentionally assume the tone of a cross-examining counsel, and of course that would end in absolute failure.

Begin with a "you will admit, Mr. Jones, that this line is in much demand" or some reference to quality, or price—then watch his face and demeanor. Perhaps he says suddenly, "Are your goods right—really?" You are surprised to hear such a question. But do not be hasty or betray a disturbed feeling. Just answer the question. Later, when you have gotten the order, go over that interview piece by piece. Ask what made him query the quality. At last you get at the truth. You were too eager in talking about "taking the goods back and returning the money." It made him begin to doubt the proposition—hence his question. At the very moment you were persuading him you unpersuaded him by a false emphasis. Rightly used, the "money back" policy is a good one, but when driven home with a hammer it defeats its own purpose, for the customer suspects there must be something wrong with the goods.

The key to the whole situation lies in this ability to get at the cause of the customer's holding aloof from action, and only questions deftly put can reveal it. Get him to say something—to offer a criticism—to ask a question—to state a case—anything to lay bare the workings of his mind. He may of course simply shrug his shoulders and say nothing: that can only mean you talked him into buying and talked him out again; or else that a new objection has occurred to him and he is now not interested enough to debate it with you. But hold on to him until you get to know what that objection is—then answer it with vim and smartness. The worst that can happen to you is to let him dismiss you until a more convenient season.' The convenient season is NOW. Gather your resources together and use them so as to turn this almost persuaded customer into a satisfied buyer.

EXERCISES

A. QUESTIONS FOR REVIEW:
 (1) What is the chief explanation of the almost persuaded customer?
 (2) How would you deal with him?
 (3) What do you mean by talking a buyer into buying and talking him out again?

B. QUESTIONS FOR WRITTEN ANSWERS:
 (1) How far is it advisable to cross-examine a customer about his hesitation to give a definite order?
 (2) A customer says: "I like your goods and the price is all right, but I can't give you an order yet." Write out a reply to this remark.

LESSON TWENTY-EIGHT
THE SALESMAN'S CATECHISM

THE object of instituting a set of questions and answers is two-fold: first, it is disciplinary; second, it is creative.

A good authority on the subject says that one of the best salesmen he ever knew went through a disciplinary catechism every morning of his life. Here it is:

Am I working for a good house? Yes.

Has my house the reputation and prestige of being one of the best in its line? Yes.

Have we made hundreds and thousands of sales like the sales I am going to make to-day? Yes.

Have we an enormous body of satisfied users? Yes.

Am I selling the best goods of the kind made anywhere in the world? Yes.

Is the price I am asking a fair one? Yes.

Do the men I am going to call on need the article I am selling? Yes.

Do they realize that now? No.

Will they all want to buy when they first see me? No.

Is that the very reason I am going to call on them—because at present they don't want my goods and haven't bought them? Yes.

Am I justified in asking a "prospect's" time and attention to present my proposition? Certainly.

Am I going to get into the office of every man I call on, if there is any earthly way to do it? I am.

Am I going to sell every man I call on to-day? Most decidedly.

There is a fine mental drill in this method and although it might not be necessary to make a daily application of it, there can be no doubt that applied at frequent intervals its influence is bound to be most beneficial.

---

125 *Brain Power Manual*, p. 144.

The other kind of catechism is intended not to *test* progress so much as to *make* it. It is creative in effect.

For instance, the salesman questions himself after this fashion:

i. Is there any method of presenting my goods which is more likely to fulfill the law of sale than the one I am using? If so, what is it?

ii. How can I improve my practice of opening out the interview?

iii. Have I thoroughly mastered the newest ideas of competing houses, and have I corresponded with my firm about them?

iv. Is my territory loaded up? Or is there room for more goods? Am I assisting my customers to sell the goods I sold to them, so as to make way for further orders?

v. What opportunity is there to develop new lines of goods, profitable in themselves and helpful to sell the older lines?

vi. Why do I possess so large a list of "almost sales?" Is there not something wrong with my methods?

vii. How can I avoid credit mistakes?

EXERCISES

A. QUESTIONS FOR REVIEW:
  (1) What two-fold value for the salesman has a series of questions and answers?
  (2) How does the constant facing of such a catechism act as a mental and moral discipline?
  (3) In what way can a series of questions suggest new ways of doing business?

B. QUESTIONS FOR WRITTEN ANSWERS:
  (1) "The asking of a question is not in itself difficult; it is the answer that is important." Comment on this statement in the light of the preceding lesson.
  (2) Write out two questions which a salesman might ask himself when he finds he cannot get interviews as readily as he used to do.

LESSON TWENTY-NINE

The Struggle with Competition

THERE are two attitudes a salesman may take up in regard to his competitors: the first is *fear* and the second is *comprehension*. To fear a competitor is as good as to give the battle up to him at once. Mr. Armour once sent out a man to sell lard. After a time the traveller wired that Swift's men were selling the stuff at a lower price. No answer was dispatched. From the next town another telegram came with similar news, and an answer was wired back suggesting he should study and sell Armour's lard, not Swift's. A very proper reply, too.

It is curious to note how fear demoralizes some men when they are dealing with the lower figures of a competitor. This is bad policy. Price-cutting is a sign of weakness in many instances, and customers encourage it because they have a shrewd notion that sooner or later the limit will be reached and the supposed inflated profits will be impossible forever after. When the goods are good and the profits reasonable, no traveller need be afraid of price-cutting, for although the struggle may go against him at the moment, he will win eventually. The customer who knows he can "squeeze" a traveller once will try to squeeze him again, and as no salesman likes to allow an order to go by, he arranges for a reduction—"just this time." The effect is bad all round, and I am not surprised to find that business houses are beginning to fix prices in such a way that the salesman cannot reduce them without the permission of the sales-manager. In such an attitude there is a feeling of dignity and business spirit which the present habit of cutting entirely lacks.

Comprehension is the right word to use in reference to your competitors. It means you are to know all about them and what they are doing. Large firms will sometimes employ a special traveller to do nothing else: he makes it his life's work to study the deeds of competing firms. He is required to note carefully the stock carried by merchants and ascertain if his firm's goods are being properly displayed; if the price is being cut; to what extent competing goods are being sold; if the salesmen sent out by his firm are selling as many goods as conditions will allow; to note carefully the kind and amount of advertising done by competitors, and especially to learn if the goods are being imitated in any way by unscrupulous people. In other words, he keeps his firm fully informed as to the actual conditions of the business.

This is not *fear;* it is real *comprehension*—an understanding of things as they are. There was once a salesman who sold toilet soap successfully for years until a competitor came upon the scene and began to offer a soap of the same size, put up as artistically, and equally well perfumed, at a lower price. The first man worked hard but began to lose ground. Then he wrote to the sales-manager, stating all the facts and asking for permission to reduce the price in order to meet competition. The sales-manager sent for him and put the two soaps on the table. The original article was cut in two and it smelt as good in the center as it did at the circumference. The new article was cut in two and had no scent at all in the center; in fact the perfume came from the wrapper and not from the soap itself. The first salesman went out on the road again and soon recovered the lost ground. Had he possessed sufficient initiative, he would have done this without the aid of the manager.

To follow the habits of the business thermometer by an up and down movement of the figures is sheer fright. If Jones raises his price, you raise yours; if you lower yours, he lowers his. Where is the sense of this skirmish with prices? It may be what is called *meeting* competition—which seems to consist in doing what others do—but it should be your aim to *beat* competition. If you are a railroad freight agent and your company quotes a fair special rate for a class of goods largely manufactured in your district but used mostly in a distant state, you repeat the quotation and solicit business, only to find another railroad is carrying the stuff at a rate which you know is not remunerative. Are you to "meet" competition by quoting the same price—one that does not pay? No. Keep calling and keep soliciting. The other company will get tired in

---

[1] Salesmanship, Vol. I, pp. 86-7.

time, for after it has paid a few heavy claims for damages and added these amounts to the daily loss (submitted to in the hope of gaining other traffic), it will be ready to raise its figures to the level of yours. Before this happens, however, it is probable that an irritating delay of a consignment will cause the firm to give you the freight, in the hope of receiving better service and more general satisfaction. But you would probably not have gotten the order, if you had not kept yourself in evidence by repeated calls.

In the higher reaches of salesmanship competition is overcome by creating new demands and supplying them. This is an advanced question that we may not go into now, but its simplest truth is this: in the older classes of goods in constant demand, competition tends to settle prices permanently, whereas in the case of the new article and the new demand, competition is eliminated for a time, at least.

EXERCISES

A. QUESTIONS FOR REVIEW:
- (1) Name the two attitudes that a salesman may take up towards his competitors.
- (2) Why is fear an emotion to be avoided?
- (3) Show how a full and complete knowledge of the competition to be faced is the only policy.

B. QUESTIONS FOR WRITTEN ANSWERS:
- (1) What effect has price-cutting on the orders of a salesman?
- (2) How would you "meet" competition?

LESSON THIRTY
"POINTERS"

EVERY salesman is furnished with a list of instructions by his sales-manager, and it should be a matter of deep concern to keep them in spirit and in letter. If one item urges the importance of making all offers for *immediate acceptance,* don't allow the customer to persuade you to wait until "next Monday" or "next week." Why? Because he may use your quotation to secure a lower price from your competitor; and, naturally, you run the risk of losing the order.

(2) Keep a record of your visits to every customer. The advantage of such a record is that when you call upon him you know what you said and did on the previous visit. It is not to be expected you can carry all this in your memory—the *substance* of it you may, but not the details—and all details are important. Some of them the customer may himself have forgotten, and it is to your benefit—and probably his own—to be able to remind him. As to the method of keeping this record, a loose-leaf pocketbook is the most serviceable.

(3) Sell your goods to yourself first. The sales-manager, knowing how desirable this is, makes an effort to arouse your enthusiasm in the proposition you are to carry round, but he cannot succeed unless you adopt the principle of self-help. By selling to yourself I mean you should create, and sustain daily, the belief in the goods you are offering to the buyer. Every morning start out with a fresh access of courage and confidence obtained from a review of the work you undertake.

(4) Be simple in your language. Sales have been lost because the salesman, having a natural liking for technicalities, indulged himself so liberally in his fondness for expression that the customer was unable to follow the selling talk. Many dealers are of foreign origin, and, although they have acquired English, it is not advanced enough to give them a mastery over technical terms. This is a special reason for simplicity, but the general advantage of

clear language ought to be sufficient to prevent the salesman from rioting in terms that convey no meaning to the hearer, and only serve to make him feel his ignorance.

(5) There is much truth in the saying that "a good salesman works on quality; a poor one on prices." I do not say price is purely secondary in a selling talk; I say that to argue prices first and last is a false move and denotes a poor salesman. Quality, on the other hand, is of first importance. If you wish to make a customer desire your goods, it is not the price that will draw him: he has to *pay* the price and you do not want to emphasize the necessity of his parting with money. You show that your goods are *superior,* and this is the item which creates the desire to possess them.

(6) The approach to a customer may contain a few generalities, but directly he turns his eyes to you, begin to talk specific *points*. Get down to hard-pan on the first opportunity. I do not mean you are to say, "I am here to sell you cutlery," or tin tacks, or whatever you represent, but to state the *points* that skillfully lead up to your cutlery or tin tacks proposition. The long introduction is useless. It is as if a man built the porch bigger than the house.

(7) Remember that there are no trifles in salesmanship. I have heard of a man who lost a large contract because he lighted a cigarette at the wrong moment. He had to deal with a "prospect" who abominated cigarettes, and by igniting one at the conclusion of a successful talk he gave the "prospect" mortal offense. It was very foolish probably on the part of the anti-cigarette person, but the salesman must be ready to conciliate prejudices. These trifles are not confined to any one sphere; they have to do with every aspect of the relationship between buyer and seller.

(8) Continually use your imagination to look at yourself and your proposition from the customer's standpoint. Put yourself in his place. Think with his mind and feel with his heart. Make his finances yours for the time being, and ask yourself what *you* would do. This habit will save you from being one-sided. It will give you new viewpoints for your selling talks, and new methods of approaching difficult people.

(9) You are a unit in a large organization and the success of the whole depends on the success of the individuals of which it is composed. It therefore depends on *you*. But you must learn to work not only as a unit but as one of a team. There is a real difference between the two. You might get together a group of fine football players, individually, but until they have played *as a team* they are not ready to compete with others who do, and who move as if they had only *one* mind. They accomplish fine results by loyalty to their captain and to each other. Let it be so in salesmanship. Work *for* your house and *with* your fellow salesman. Play the game, by being loyal to every rule of order. Uphold the house and the house will uphold you.

(10) Keep the idea of *service* ever before you, and you can't go wrong. Never identify yourself with a firm which aims to make money on the *anyhow* system. And when you have found a right firm, never get an order by misrepresentation, or by holding back important details. The customer should know everything about the goods, and the conditions of sale; he should be treated in such a way that on leaving him you can honestly say you have done him a good turn.

EXERCISES

A. QUESTIONS FOR REVIEW:
  (1) How many aspects of a salesman's duties are dealt with in this lesson? Name them.
  (2) On what point does a good salesman lay special emphasis?
  (3) How does imagination help a salesman?

B. QUESTIONS FOR WRITTEN ANSWERS:
  (1) A sales-manager said, "I sell my goods to my travellers first." On what does his success in this work depend?
  (2) Explain the need of observing trifles in (a) dress and (b) speech.

E

**PRACTICAL LESSONS IN
SPECIALTY SELLING**

LESSON THIRTY-ONE
ON SPECIALTY SELLING

THE specialty salesman differs from wholesale salesmen in selling his goods direct to the user. He may offer pianolas, books, sewing-machines, typewriters, bonds, or a hundred different articles, but he offers them to the individual and not to the trade. The commercial traveller, by way of contrast, has a regular line of customers (after he has built up his trade), it being his duty to add to that list as rapidly as possible. In the case of the retail salesman the customers come to him. Each of these two classes has a big advantage over the third class, the specialty salesman, because, as a rule, the latter has to find a new customer every time he makes a sale.

To illustrate: the insurance salesman is very seldom able to sell any one person more than one insurance policy. Occasionally he may succeed, but the chances of a second sale are by the very nature of the transaction not as great as in the case of the commercial traveller or the retail salesman. The same is true of the book salesman, those who sell investment securities and those who sell novelties from door to door.

The business of finding the customer, then, is important, but there are other items equally important, and to each of them I shall give as full a treatment as space will allow. The divisions of the subject are these:

1. The article to be sold.
2. How to sell it.
3. And where.

I shall show the wisdom of selecting an article which is right in itself and right in its relation to the salesman. The temptation to take up "fake" goods carrying large profits is great—at least, it is so to those men whose minds are not imbued wtih the idea of *service*. Unless you can meet the purchaser again and look him honestly in the face, you had better not sell at all, for "fakes" do no good to the seller and they are a fraud committed on the buyer.

"How to sell" brings us once more to the principles already noticed, for all selling has the same psychological basis. However, each department of the business has its own special methods, and these will be noticed in due course. We shall find that in this connection we have to study the customer in all his phases and determine how the goods are related to his needs.

On the subject of where to find customers, the specialty salesman must be more than ordinarily proficient, for, as I have stated, it is in this respect that his work differs most from that of other salesmen. He is a scout in the fullest sense of the term and must see orders when other men less trained can detect no sign of possible business. Although for the time confined to a prescribed territory, he must know that territory from centre to circumference, not merely as a portion of the planet's surface but as a place where men and women live who may be buyers of his goods.

EXERCISES

A. QUESTIONS FOR REVIEW:
   (1) Distinguish the specialty man from the man who travels for a wholesaler.
   (2) What are the three questions ever before the specialty man?
   (3) What is his most important duty? Why?

B. QUESTIONS FOR WRITTEN ANSWERS:
   (1) How would you dissuade a man from selling "fake" goods? Write a brief letter embodying your arguments.
   (2) If you were asked to say whether or not you preferred to be a specialty salesman, what reasons would you urge for and against.

LESSON THIRTY-TWO
The Importance of Selecting the Right Article

TO succeed in specialty selling it is necessary that you select (1) something good, and (2) something you can believe in—something into which you can throw your whole soul. The two are not identical. You may select a good typewriter, but unless it appeals to your feelings as well as your judgment, you are not likely to succeed to any great extent as a salesman, because your logic lacks the advantage of enthusiasm.

The point is one on which I wish to dwell because of its real importance. Here are two salesmen, A and B, who are equally convinced about the merits of a new pencil-sharpener. B is thoroughly persuaded that it is good, cheap, and a certain seller. A is of the same opinion, but he looks at the article from a different viewpoint, or rather he surrounds it with emotion. To him it is not only a clever device: it is an article that awakens *feeling*—it will render a great service to the buyer. Listen to his selling talk and you will detect a forcefulness which is absent from the selling talk of B who addresses himself to a series of argumentative proofs. I do not say B may not be a good salesman; I am drawing attention to the advantage which A has over B because A not only believes with his mind but with his heart; he is an enthusiast. He is ready to talk about that device, even though no sale may be in prospect.

This feeling is something very difficult to feign, and in salesmanship it is not alone what you say but how you say it and how deeply you *feel* it, that carries conviction to the mind of the listener. Enthusiasm is one of the prime requisites of success in the power of persuasion growing out of your desire to serve; and it is difficult for any one to be genuinely enthusiastic unless he loves his work.

Why is it that A has developed for the pencil-sharpener a feeling that B does not possess? Probably because he has a native liking for mechanical things. On the other hand, B may feel a similar attraction to literary productions, and his true place is in selling books, not instruments. Let him find a set of volumes containing the life story of our Presidents and he will become as enthusiastic as A is about the ingenuity and usefulness of the pencil-sharpener. Put A to the selling of the volumes and the probability is he would be convinced of their value, but, his natural leanings being in another direction, he would offer them minus the subtle joy and confidence he reposed in the mechanical device.

Thus you see that to get something right to sell is not enough; you must get the thing which is right *for you*. This is a matter to be decided by your own judgment and feeling; nobody else can decide it for you. Don't be in a hurry to select the first thing that comes to your notice, unless time and circumstances leave you no option. Wait for the one article that will appeal to reason and emotion alike. You might be successful as a bond salesman, but only moderately so as a seller of life insurance; and you might be most successful of all as the representative of a house disposing of a new rubber heel. Of course not every man gets into the right place the first time, but a little watchfulness and patience will ultimately land you in the sphere where you can do full justice to your powers.

EXERCISES

A. QUESTIONS FOR REVIEW:
  (1) What are the two rules in selecting an article to sell?
  (2) How does *feeling* affect the selling of an article?
  (3) What is the difference between a mind that is logically convinced and one that is not only convinced but enthusiastic?

B. QUESTIONS FOR WRITTEN ANSWERS:
  (1) What is the result of a good man's choice of an unsuitable line of goods?
  (2) Give an illustration of the right article's being sold by the wrong man. Assign a suitable article to him—one that will make him the "right" man.
  (Study the example in the lesson.)

LESSON THIRTY-THREE
How to Analyze the Article

WHAT knowledge of the article to be sold ought the salesman to possess and how ought he to make the best use of it in effecting sales? In other words, to what extent and in what particulars should the salesman be informed respecting his goods and the goods of his competitors?

It is difficult to formulate principles and give definite rules regarding the kind and extent of knowledge salesmen in every line should possess respecting their goods, but one rule always holds good:

If possible, know more about your article and its competing value than does your customer or your competitor—not necessarily to tire or bewilder your customer in the selling talk, but as a magazine of reserve power that can readily be drawn upon, should occasion demand it.

Below I give a list of questions to be asked about the goods you have determined to sell.

1. What is the article?
2. What is it for?
3. Of what is it made?
4. What do the raw materials cost?
5. Where are they procured?
6. What is the cost of manufacture?
7. What is the cost when delivered to the customer?
8. How does the price asked compare with competitors' prices?
9. Who are the most likely customers?
10. Where can I find them?
11. Is the article a luxury or a necessity?
12. What is its history?
13. How does that history affect the selling talk?
14. What advantages has this article over that of rival houses?

15. How is the sale of this article affected by times and seasons?
16. What is the size of the average order?
17. How do jobbers come in?
18. Are commission charges heavy?
19. What changes in style are pending?

It looks rather formidable, does it not? And yet it is quite simple. Some of the sections, for certain articles, like bonds or educational courses, would hardly be available, and yet they would for others; the scheme is adaptable to every class of goods. I give on the opposite page a complete analysis to show how it works out.

This will explain satisfactorily the method of analysis and the reason why it should be carried out. One great mistake made by many so-called salesmen is their conceited belief that all they need is samples. These are sometimes defined as "specimens of the goods our house manufactures, and necessary in order to excite the interest of prospective customers and convince them of the high quality of the goods for which we expect them to pay their money."

That definition does not go far enough. Don't put your house and the quality of its goods foremost! The customer is far more interested in his own affairs than in yours. Show him, therefore, how his needs are satisfied by your article, and he will listen to you.

As far as possible analyze in the same way, the goods of your competitor. The customers to whom you appeal are sure to study them, and you must not be behind them in your knowledge of the trade. The idea is not to attack "the other fellow's" article, be it a book, a patent medicine, a piano-player or what not; it is to have knowledge and be prepared to answer objections arising in connection with the price, mechanism, use, or some other point of debate. I regard it as wise to speak well of a competitor's goods in a general sort of way; but it is very pleasant and profitable to be able to say of a rival proposition: "That is quite true; I cheerfully admit the merits of the goods you mention, but"— and then proceed to show with exactness the points of superiority in your own articles. You cannot do this unless you have first analyzed your own goods completely and in like manner studied the goods of your competitor.

Analysis of Sale of Enrollment in the Sheldon School

Enrollment of the Student the Desired End.
- 1. Instruction.
  - 1. Matter.
    1. Man-building or Self-development.
    2. Character Analysis.
    3. Business Logic.
    4. Business Psychology.
    5. General Business Topics.
  - 2. Features.
    1. Simple.
    2. Interesting.
    3. Practical.
    4. Uplifting.
  - 3. Medium— The Sheldon School.
    1. Sheldon Lessons.
    2. Text-books.
    3. Correspondence and Business Counsel.
    4. Membership in Study Club with other Students.
  - 4. Fruits.
    1. Business capacity.
    2. Increased earnings.
    3. Improved personality.
    4. Happiness in life.
- 2. Student.
  - 1. Necessity.
    1. Fulfills ambition.
    2. Develops powers.
    3. Gains promotion.
    4. Self-growth.
  - 2. Facility.
    1. Scholarship not needed.
    2. Teaching method simple.
    3. Leisure hour study.
    4. Can study anywhere.
  - 3. Advantages.
    1. Ability.
    2. Reliability.
    3. Endurance.
    4. Action.
  - 4. Action.
    1. You are capable.
    2. Employers want you.
    3. Success is certain.
    4. Now the proper time.

This means business; it means hard work it is true, but it also means profit. It means a higher salary or increased commissions; sometimes it means, eventually, a managership or proprietorship.

EXERCISES

A. QUESTIONS FOR REVIEW:
    (1) Why is it important to know all about the goods?
    (2) You are to know more about them than other people: Who, especially, are those people?
    (3) Why would you deem it desirable to analyze the competitor's goods?

B. QUESTIONS FOR WRITTEN ANSWERS:
    (1) and (2) Write an analysis of this text-book.

LESSON THIRTY-FOUR

THINKING OUT A SELLING TALK

ON referring to Lesson Eight we are reminded of the four mental factors of a sale—attention, interest, desire, and action. Your object as a specialty salesman is to get the customer to buy your goods, and to do so you must fulfill the mental law of sale.

The selling talk, in its make-up, is determined by the need of first securing favorable attention; after that the effort is to create an interest in the proposition; then to arouse desire; and finally to obtain a decision to purchase.

Very often more than one selling talk is necessary to dispose of an article; for, although you have obtained a favorable hearing for perhaps five minutes, the prospective customer may deflect you from your course by an objection with more or less reason in it, and you have to be prepared on the instant to reply and to take up the point in a secondary talk. Perhaps a third talk will be needed ere you are successful.

But remember this: the purpose of each talk is to make a sale, and as you want to do this as early as possible, the first selling talk should be the strongest. It is true you have two others behind it, each adequate for the same result, but they are in the nature of reserves and should not be called into action unless circumstances demand it. Experience proves that in the making of initial customers, and in the case of bringing back into line dissatisfied customers, only a small percentage give their first orders or renew their patronage on the first selling talk. Nevertheless, you should rigidly ignore this fact until it is forced upon you.

Before you begin your first selling talk you must draw the customer's attention; and as attention comes through knowledge, and knowledge is gained through the senses, it is well to decide beforehand the best methods of approach. Imagine the different kinds of men and women to whom you will address your proposition, and ask yourself the question, "How ought I to introduce it?" You will not think very long before you find yourself in possession of a considerable variety of suggestions.

One safe rule is to appeal to as many of the customer's senses as possible. A neat appearance and a cheery voice appeal to his vision and hearing, and through them to his judgment or his prejudices. A man selling a new cereal once gained my attention by handing me a few kernels and asking me to taste them; and another salesman selling books used to hand the prospective customer a bound volume, asking him to smell it, and saying, "You can easily discern that to be genuine leather." This is rather precipitous and would not succeed with every salesman, but it was an appeal to sight, touch and smell.

Think out your attention-getters and make a list of them. Keep the list in your pocket and study it occasionally. Common sense and experience will teach you how to use it. It is a cardinal rule that your first talk should be general in its nature—like the sketch of a picture—allowing the main selling points to stand out in bold relief. At the outset be careful to select from your points one that the mind of the customer can readily grasp, one to which his mind can readily assent, one that you feel sure will be interesting. Then see to it that the next point you advance is related to the first, and so with the third, fourth and fifth, each naturally fitting into the point ahead of it and the point behind it, until you have completed a scientific description of your goods or proposition.

Force the wedge in gently. Be modest and moderate in your claims at the start. Make only such statements as will be accepted by your customer without demur. In this way you get him into the habit of agreeing with you.

Be brief: you must avoid giving the impression that you are likely to take up too much of your customer's valuable time, or that you are likely to confuse him with a mass of details. The difficulty with many specialty men, to put it in plain Saxon, is that they do not know when to stop. But a man who constructs a first selling talk on the lines suggested, arranges for a climax—to give the customer an opportunity to decide. In the words of a good business man, he has observed the three principles: first, have something to say; second, say it; and third, quit talking.

Now by ceasing to talk I do not mean silence; I mean that the salesman will probably produce the document with "the dotted line" and ask for the customer's initials; or ask whether he will take advantage of the discount terms which may be offered. Avoid awkward pauses, for if the customer makes no sign, begin with the second talk, or enlarge on one of the features of the first.

The memorizing of a talk is advisable, but only when it has been proved to be effective after two or three experiments. It is poor policy to commit to memory a set of so-called selling phrases that accomplish nothing! Analyze the goods, analyze the customer, write down what you wish to say, and try it out to see how it works. If it promises well, memorize it; if not, alter it until it does.

The formal (but not necessarily uninteresting) recital of the merits and uses of your goods gives a fluency to your speech that is highly advantageous, because it enables you to secure the attention and interest of the customer in spite of himself. Not that you sell him the article against his will, but that your unhesitating explanation provides him with no opportunity to skirmish against your proposition—and afterwards, when he is a satisfied purchaser, he bears you no grudge because you thus outgeneraled him—probably he places it to your credit.

"But how about interruptions?" some one will ask. "What am I to do, if the customer stops me with a sharp question?"

There is no rule that can be applied in a mechanical manner to all interruptions, but herein lies the advantage of a skillful and interesting method of presenting a proposition: it tends to prevent the customer from interposing a remark, because the personality and the selling power of the salesman enable him to "hold the floor." But when interrupting questions are asked, as they often are, try to turn them to advantage.

If the question should be about a minor detail, answer it rapidly, and continue without appearing to notice the interposition. If it should be rather determined, answer it carefully with a smile, then proceed with an "as I was saying"—

Never show that you resent these enforced gaps in your presentation. A mischievous buyer will sometimes throw in an objection or two to spoil your efforts, and will be quite pleased if you lose your temper or show the slightest sign of impatience; but if you conquer by tact, he will respect your powers all the more and be inclined to sign the order form.

The function of the second and third selling talk is to continue the arguments of the first when those arguments have for the moment proved unavailing. Of course the customer knows nothing about your first, second and third: to him it is all one talk—with a few interruptions. But when your first attempt does not end in a deal you know at once you have not aroused sufficient interest and desire, consequently you are to fall back upon the second talk, which is specially drawn up to serve this purpose. You go into greater detail; become more positive in tone; you suggest that the customer agrees with you.

The function of the third talk is to deal with a man who is confessedly a difficult subject, otherwise he would have decided to make a purchase after hearing the other two. Presumably these talks created some interest and aroused some desire, but not enough to cause action, wherefore the third talk should be one that puts all its strength into decision-making. You will have to fight objections with cleverness and good humor, by agreeing with the objector—from *his* point of view, but showing him tactfully where that is wrong. You will press the argument from advantage, and when you feel the psychological moment has arrived—there is no other way of knowing it than by *feeling* it—you will confidently act as if the sale were completed and get the customer's name on your order form.

The successful handling of a third selling talk is a test of the salesman's natural ability, and of the versatility arising out of a solid preparation for his work. It is the time for surprises in the form of new objections and unexpected attacks. But this element is not continuous, for after being on the road a few months a salesman soon knows what he may expect to meet and is ready for it.

THE ART OF SELLING

This brief review will give the inexperienced salesman some idea of the need of intelligent preparation for his work. He cannot be too careful in analyzing his goods or his possible customers; and he cannot be too careful in composing his selling talks. Persuading a man to buy is not a hypnotic process, as some people incorrectly imagine; it is the result of knowledge skillfully applied, and there is not a symptom of mental magic in it from the first word to the last.

EXERCISES.

A. QUESTIONS FOR REVIEW:
 (1) What need determines the make-up of the selling talk?
 (2) Why should there be more than one?
 (3) Describe the functions of each.

B. QUESTIONS FOR WRITTEN ANSWERS:
 (1) If you were constructing a selling talk for a new typewriter, what would be your first aim, and having decided it, how would you realize it?
 (2) How does a good salesman deal with interruptions?

LESSON THIRTY-FIVE
GEOGRAPHY FOR SPECIALTY SALESMEN

THE question of *where* to find the customer is one that is answered, partially at least, by the sales-manager, who appoints his men to a specific territory, outside the radius of which they must not go. But the finding of the customer, even within the radius, is no small matter, for although the obvious purchasers are easily discovered, there are scores of others who have to be sought diligently. Here is an opportunity for showing your power of initiative.

A little thought will prove to you that it is your duty, not only to yourself but to your employers to see everybody, if you are selling an article that naturally appeals to everybody. Remember, please, that in this twentieth century there are great numbers of independent women. And while there are very many wives who, either through necessity or choice, consult their husbands in nearly every purchase, there are thousands who are entirely independent and really at liberty to purchase what they please, within the limits of their finances. The specialty salesman who overlooks this point and through false pride will not ring a door-bell, is, to say the least, very short-sighted. Your motto should be, "see everybody," and then stick to your motto. The best specialty salesmen I know, who sell articles of the class which would appeal to everybody, make it a rule to canvass the business end of a town first; but they don't stop there. Having visited every store, every office, every factory and other place where it is at all possible to find and see a man, they then start out on a systematic house to house, street by street canvass of the residence district. In doing this they find many men at home—usually accessible only in the daytime, because they work at night. They meet others, too, who are men of leisure, and they find very many women, who, as a rule, are more susceptible to salesmanship than are the men. This is true from the very nature of things. A man, especially if he is a business man, is oftentimes very much occupied with his own affairs. It is usually much more difficult to interrupt Mr.

Brown and get his attention than it is to interest Mrs. Brown. If he is a very successful man, the chances, as already stated, are that he is a very busy man; but if he is a very successful man, it then follows that Mrs. Brown is not a very busy woman. She may be entirely a lady of leisure. If Mr. Brown is very busy, and therefore very successful, the prospects are that Mrs. Brown has plenty of pin-money. Do you not see where the logic of the situation naturally leads us?

In my own experience in specialty salesmanship I had it brought home to me frequently how true it is that we cannot tell "where lightning is going to strike." Many of my best orders have been booked in houses where, judging from outward appearances, one would scarcely expect to get orders at all! Again, I found it was the only way to insure getting all the business—in other words, in order to find all the customers that there are in any given territory, be it big or small, is to see everybody, see everybody, see everybody!

MAKE FRIENDS WITH THE CHILDREN. It is through them oftentimes that you get hold of the heart-strings of the mother and the father.

Personally I have made it a point not to sell to some people though I knew it was within my power to do so. I refer to cases of evident poverty or, at least, straitened circumstances. You strengthen yourself infinitely in your own estimation, in your own inner consciousness of right, by doing right. You must be careful not to carry this principle to the extreme and not to take the people's word for it when they say "I can't afford it." You must be the judge in that matter. People get into the habit of saying "I can't afford it," and even say that when they really can afford it. They may not really mean to misrepresent, but they say it from force of habit. If your intuition or your judgment tells you that they can afford to buy it, then proceed with the firm resolution to convince them that they can afford it. This resolution and the power of your conviction are infinitely strengthened by your having been honest with yourself in every case where you did not press for a sale, feeling in your own heart that it would be wrong for you to make the sale, even if you could. After having thus fortified yourself, being clad in the armor of justice, righteousness (in the sense of *rightness*), you can fight battles which you are sure to win; and in the long run you will find infinitely more people who can afford that which you have to sell than those who cannot afford it. Thousands of people have been thankful later that they yielded to the persistency of solicitors and purchased different articles, which at the beginning of the conversation they had stated positively they did not want or could not afford.

Please do not misunderstand me in the instructions just given. The solicitor who is too much amenable to the suggestion lurking in the comments of his customers who is easily put off—believes his "prospects" when they tell him that they cannot afford to buy, will never make a success as a salesman. But on the other hand, neither will the solicitor gain the highest heights possible to be attained, if he unscrupulously forces sales, regardless of rights or conscience. There is a happy medium to be arrived at only through the exercise of keen intuition and correct judgment.

If the foregoing instructions are followed, it will be apparent to you that it is possible for the specialty salesman to take a given field and work it over and over again, and oftentimes the second and third, and even the fourth and fifth workings of the field prove to be more profitable than the first one. This is especially true in the sale of perishable articles.

I once knew a very successful specialty salesman who was working at Eureka, California. This town is located on the coast north of San Francisco, in Humboldt county. The salesman had worked that town with moderate success, although anything but satisfactorily. Across the bay from Eureka was located the little town of Arcata. It could be reached by boat in half an hour or such a matter, but a wagon-road led to it around the bay a distance of some twenty or thirty miles. Along this road were fruit ranches and back of it were lumber-camps which employed men at good wages. It was in the rainy season and the mud was deep. The natural thing to do, or at least what most salesmen would have done, was to go by boat across to Arcata; but this salesman was out after business. He believed in going out of the beaten paths of other salesmen. He believed in going to places where lazy salesmen didn't go, and so he walked to Arcata. He visited the fruit ranches and tramped up the side roads to the lumber-camps. He was selling a book priced at $5.75 a copy and had been placing about three copies a day in Eureka; but in one day on this trip around the bay he sold twenty-two copies and reached Arcata with a total of over 100 sales, upon which the profits were over $200.

Another illustration: A specialty salesman was once working in Escanaba, Michigan. He had worked the town quite thoroughly, both the business and residence districts. Certain friends, whose acquaintance he had made while at work there, advised him strongly to go on to the copper country, Houghton and Hancock; but he knew this was just what other salesmen ahead of him had done and he began to inquire about the immediate neighborhood. The postmaster told him of a little town called Ford River a few miles distant. It was a little hamlet of only three or four hundred people—nearly all employed by the Ford River Lumber Co. He was selling an encyclopædia the price of which was from $40.00 to $60.00. Some of his friends told him that those people would not buy an encyclopædia, but he believed in thorough work. That territory had been assigned to him—it was his duty to get out of it all there was in it, and as it was his policy to go out of the beaten path, he drove over to Ford River. His livery bill was $2.00, but on goods which he sold in Ford River he made $150.00, because he placed fifteen sets of volumes yielding an average commission of $10.00 cash. Partially, though not wholly, to his surprise, he found that he was the first encyclopædia agent who had ever visited that little village. The lessons of these illustrations are too obvious to need comment. Get out of the beaten path! It is to your interest as well as to the interest of your employer to work your territory by the square inch; squeeze the lemon until it is dry. Drag your field enough, and then drag it once more.

Many specialty salesmen labor under the delusion that they can do nothing in the holiday season; and many imagine that the summer is a very bad time to work and a most excellent time to loaf. These are in the main purely mental conditions. It is all in the way you look at it. If you employ the imagination to create adverse conditions, then the conditions are adverse as far as you are concerned. The adversity is a reality. If, on the other hand, you reason on the subject, you can employ the imagination to call up pleasant mental pictures of the possibilities at these seasons. Reason after this fashion: The majority of specialty salesmen, the ordinary solicitors, are loafing at this time. This leaves the coast clear for me. I believe it is about the best time of the whole year for me to hustle. Competition is less keen. It shall be with me a case of the early bird catching the worm. The Christmas and New Year season finds people in a cheerful mood. The spirit of brotherly love is abroad in the land. I shall employ this to my advantage. I shall make the biggest record of my entire year during this holiday season, etc., etc.

One of the most successful specialty salesmen that I know told me only recently that during the last holiday season he made the greatest number of daily sales of the entire year; and he did it by canvassing himself into just this mental attitude. He created an ideal in his own mind and then made the ideal a reality by virtue of his enthusiasm and his hustle.

This man argues with himself the same way in summer time. He reasons that this is when most specialty salesmen are loafiing. Then he says to himself that he will make hay while the sun shines, and he hustles and gets the business.

It is a fact that during the summer season business men as a rule are less rushed than they are in the fall, in winter and in spring. They have more time to talk. It is easy enough to find chances, if you look for them, but there is nothing quite so easy to find in all the world as trouble and imaginary difficulties, if you are really looking for them. Don't look for trouble! "Never trouble trouble till trouble troubles you." Remember the great rule of life that nearly every seeming disadvantage can be converted into a real advantage. Just simply turn things around and make them come your way.

The expert specialty salesman finds many customers by reference from one to another. When you have made a sale, don't be in too big a hurry to get away! Don't feel that your work is finished as far as that sale is concerned when you have the name on "the dotted line." A satisfied customer in specialty salesmanship should always be made the stepping-stone to another. Get references and letters of introduction where you can; get testimonial letters. It is all important in specialty salesmanship that you make good deliveries as well as many sales; and the good delivery part depends almost wholly upon how well the order is taken. This depends fully as much upon what you say after the order is booked as upon what you say before you have it booked. A customer not satisfied, or one to whom you have sold but to whom you cannot deliver, is anything but a business-getter for you. Give him such suggestions as this: "I know you are going to be delighted with this purchase. You can readily understand that my success depends upon pleasing people. I want you to be so thoroughly pleased that you will recommend this to all your friends, and I know you are going to do that for me, Mr. Brown." And then, "By the way, who are some of your friends whom you would like to have me see and who you think would appreciate this article," etc., etc. A few words tactfully put about prompt payment for goods sold on the installment plan will help the collection department immensely. Do not let your thoughts stop with the collection of your commissions only; consider also your employer's interests. This will help you as well as him. The more prosperous he is, the better he can afford to do by you. Remember always that salesmanship is the sale of goods for profit.

EXERCISES

A. QUESTIONS FOR REVIEW:
   (1) Why is it wise to give special attention to women buyers?
   (2) What do you think as to pressing a sale on *every* person you canvass?
   (3) What is the value of getting away from the beaten path?

B. QUESTIONS FOR WRITTEN ANSWERS:
   (1) Is the holiday season argument a substantial one? Argue the point.
   (2) Show how the finding of the customer calls for initiative.

LESSON THIRTY-SIX
PRACTICAL HINTS

IF you should ever be engaged as a specialty salesman on a basis that allows the charging of expenses, be scrupulously honest in rendering this account. Don't charge up at fifty cents the meal for which you paid only twenty-five! When you walk from a depot to your hotel, or *vice versa,* don't put down such an item as "Bus fare, twenty-five cents"! This habit is called "padding the account," and unfortunately it is practised by many men who ought to know better, and whose example is extremely detrimental to the beginner. A word to the wise, however, is sufficient; and when I tell you I know men who have lost promotions to salaries of $5,000 a year because they were known to be "padding," you will realize the importance of strict honesty.

(2) You should communicate with your firm every day if practicable. Let your orders and reports be neat and accurate, and if you have any suggestions to offer, be brief and to the point. Write legibly, for time is valuable, both to the sales-manager and to you. Besides, a slovenly written order may result in a serious mistake in consignment, occasioning trouble to the customer, the firm, and everybody connected with the transaction.

(3) Live well and dress well, without extravagance in either item. Be thrifty but not stingy. Many specialty men earn incomes ranging from ten to twenty thousand dollars a year, but somehow they manage to spend it all. They act as if their incomes would last forever. Figure out, early in your career, how much you can *save* without being miserly—then defend that money against all comers. You will find you have to defend it against yourself more often than anybody else.

(4) Aim at the best, both in methods and results. Do not be content with a fair average. Review occasionally a day's transactions and ask, "Was this, or that, or the other a really good sale?" "How could it have been improved?" "Am I making progress as rapidly as I should?" "Do I bore customers by talking

THE ART OF SELLING

too long after having made a sale?" Such questions go to the root of the matter, and by drawing up a set of keen questions of your own you will soon be able to analyze what you do.

(5) Make each day right and the whole year will then be right. When I began as a specialty salesman I kept my daily figures in a memorandum-book, and at the close of a two years' trip which took me 3,000 miles from home I could tell from my book exactly how every working hour had been spent and with what results.

At the beginning my entries read about as follows:

MORNING

Hours Worked.	Calls Made.	Selling Talks.	Orders Taken.
9 to 10	3	2	0
10 to 11	2	4	0

AFTERNOON

2 to 3	5	1	1
3 to 4	3	1	0
4 to 5	3	1	0
5	16	10	1

Some days in my early experience I made better records than the above, and some days I didn't work at all—I imagined I was not feeling well. At length one day I figured out my averages and discovered that my earnings had reached about a dollar an hour for the hours I actually worked. But the figures also disclosed to me that I had worked on an average only five and one-half hours a day—not much more than the office hours of a pampered bureaucrat!

This was something of an "eye-opener" to me, and I began to wonder if it were possible to keep up my hourly average of earnings in case I should increase the number of working hours. On the presumption that this would be so I figured what I might have earned by working ten hours a day instead of five and one-half hours. Again I figured what this rate of increase would amount to in a year, and then in ten years, and the totals were so dazzling that I resolved then and there I could not afford to waste so many precious hours for a long time to come—providing, of course, that my average hourly earnings were maintained for the additional working hours.

At this time my health was really poor and on that account I had partially excused myself, but now I began to care for it systematically and also to force myself to stick to the work, no matter how much I might yearn to quit and go to my room. Very soon I managed by this means to add to the daily number of my work-hours, as well as to my proficiency in the work itself, and then I began to make records somewhat like this:

MORNING

Hours Worked.	Calls Made.	Selling Talks.	Orders Taken.
8 to 9	2	1	1
9 to 10	5	2	0
10 to 11	3	2	1
11 to 12	4	2	0

AFTERNOON

2 to 3	4	3	1
3 to 4	5	3	0
4 to 5	3	2	1
5 to 6	4	2	0
8	30	17	4

But here came another pleasant surprise. After pushing my daily average up to eight working hours and keeping at that pace for a reasonable time, I found that my earnings per hour had increased rather than lessened. It was a clear example of the truth unfolded to you a little way back, that practice makes for greater skill in selling as in other arts. Hence I forced myself up to a ten-hour working standard and still found my earnings per hour to be on the increase.

Of course there is a limit to one's endurance in continued work of this kind, but under the discipline of my daily and hourly record I at length advanced to a stage where my report for weeks at a time ran about as follows for an average day's work:

MORNING

Hours Worked.	Calls Made.	Selling Talks.	Orders Taken.
8 to 9	3	2	1
9 to 10	5	3	2
10 to 11	4	2	1
11 to 12	2	2	2

AFTERNOON.

1 to 2	2	2	0
2 to 3	3	3	1
3 to 4	5	2	1
4 to 5	4	2	1
5 to 6	6	2	2

EVENING CALLS

7 to 8	2	2	2
8 to 9	3	2	1
11	39	24	14

I think my best day's record footed up "Hours Worked, 14; Calls, 36; Selling Talks, 30, and Orders Taken, 22."

It is needless that I should dwell extensively on the lesson to be drawn from the above tables. There is a common saying that "figures do not lie," and the truth that shines in these figures embodies several important teachings. In the first place it shows the advantage of keeping an exact and detailed record; the salesman can observe his progress or his shortcomings, either for comfort or correction, as the need may be. In this case it exhibits forcibly the benefits of steadfast devotion to the actual work of selling: every increase in practice was a gain both in income and capacity. Finally it is a warning against the waste of precious time, since it shows that the hours and half-hours we fritter away so heedlessly may all be turned to profitable account—profit to character and mentality no less than profit in money and business advancement. I might even add profit in health, for health is more improved through sturdy and continuous action than it could be by dawdling or doctoring.

Among my cherished maxims on this subject of the value of time I had the following: "Lost somewhere between sunrise and sunset, two golden hours, each set with sixty diamond minutes. No reward is offered, for they are gone forever!" And the resolve which I drew from this was, "I shall not lose any of my golden hours, for I really can't afford to do so."

A. QUESTIONS FOR REVIEW:

(1) With what topics do the foregoing practical hints concern themselves?
(2) Prove the importance of thrifty habits.
(3) Show how diligence as exemplified in the daily returns creates and realizes new opportunities.

B. QUESTIONS FOR WRITTEN ANSWERS:

(1) Argue a case against a salesman who is guilty of "padding his account."
(2) What is the value of a systematic record of daily results?

F
PROMOTION SALESMANSHIP

LESSON THIRTY-SEVEN
PROMOTION AND SALESMANSHIP

MY object in this lesson, and the one that follows, is to show you how the promoter is a salesman, and to analyze the goods he offers to his friends or the public.

Promotion means the financing of an enterprise—usually by selling an interest in it to a number of outsiders who expect to receive a certain amount of money per annum for the use of their capital. They become stockholders in the concern that the promotion brings into existence, or which it forms from businesses that were already engaged in trade.

There are three requisites in every promotion: (1) the promoter; (2) the investor; and (3) the enterprise. The goods offered for sale are shares in the enterprise; the buyer is the investor; and the salesman is the promoter.

In one respect, however, he is different from every other kind of salesman, for, in a real sense, he may be said to manufacture his own goods. If he be an honest man, the goods will be good; if not, they will be comparatively (if not wholly) worthless, and that is one reason why the professional promoter is often in bad odor: he does not serve the public—he exploits them for his own advantage.

I will, however, take an illustration from the work of an honest promoter, of whom there are many. Looking around him he sees a promising business handicapped for the want of capital, or a few small firms manufacturing the same article but engaged in undercutting prices until the margin of profit is almost nil. I will suppose that he turns his attention to this little group fighting a fierce competitive battle. He thinks that, if they were amalgamated and supplied with more working capital, a splendid success would result. He therefore sounds the principals of the separate concerns and finds that they are quite willing to end the strife by an equitable arrangement. The promoter's duty is to think out such an arrangement, fix the terms for doing this service, then set the scheme going and finally dispose of the stock created to supply additional working capital. That is where salesmanship comes in, but you will see in what sense he may be said to have manufactured his own goods.

The customer, that is, the investor, may be a friend of the promoter or he may be an entire stranger. If the former, the selling of the stock is purely a matter of arrangement; if the latter, other methods will have to be adopted, as I shall show in a later paragraph.

The customer's mind, during a purchase, passes through the four stages we have already noticed—attention, interest, desire and action, but greater skill is needed than in any other form of salesmanship to secure favorable attention. To part with $500.00, sometimes much more, sometimes less, is a proceeding that requires deliberation, and this the investor is not willing to give unless the proposition is one about which he knows something already, for his money is earning interest in the bank, and it needs a very attractive proposition to make him even *think* of withdrawing it.

The power of salesmanship, in promotion, lies in the name and reputation of the promoter. If his previous promotions have netted large profits to the stockholders his name is the best selling asset of a later project—indeed, it may be the only selling agency required. On the other hand, investors are as often as not asked to put their money into schemes about which they know nothing until they are informed by the promoter.

It frequently happens that an enterprise cannot be financed among friends. It may be too large an undertaking for local investors, in which event an appeal must be made elsewhere. Perhaps the promoter-salesman tries to find the money by selling the stock to a few wealthy men in the city; or he may consult a financial agent who has a clientele of investors on his list ready to take up the stock of a really promising concern.

If these efforts should fail, recourse may be had to the preparing of a more elaborate prospectus, setting forth the aims of the new corporation and supplying the names of those who direct its affairs; the business accounts for the past, together with future prospects are produced, and the selling talk winds up with an invitation to subscribe for stock.

This prospectus is advertised in the press, and sent by mail, with a covering letter, to lists of investors. Only large propositions are able to stand the expense of all this printing, advertising, and postage. Besides, the results are often so poor that as a method of disposing of stock it is going out of date except in special types of business organization. It is estimated that in an ordinary successful advertising campaign at least one dollar is expended for every dollar finally secured for the work of the enterprise. That is, in order to secure $40,000.00 by this method it will be necessary to expend not less than $20,000.00.

Selling stock by circularizing and letter writing, with only a small appropriation for advertising, is a more practised method, and it has one great advantage: it can be tested on a small scale if desired. The results on 500 letters with circulars will tell the promoter what he may expect from 5,000 or 15,000. If the returns are good the campaign may be pursued on those lines; if not, the program may be changed without incurring a great deal of expense.

The salesman is paid for his services in one of several different ways. It may be agreed that he shall have a specific sum in cash plus a number of shares; he may receive a percentage on the amount of stock sold among his friends, or, through his instrumentality, among strangers; he may dispose of the business in its entirety to another company, or he may introduce the proposition to a financial syndicate and receive from them a commission according to agreement. The amount varies from five per cent to forty and fifty per cent in mere speculative undertakings—the floating of a mining corporation, for instance.

Sometimes, in order to prevent any mishap the promoter *underwrites* all the stock before it is offered to the public. The underwriters—a syndicate of responsible financiers who specialize in this kind of work—agree, on certain conditions, to buy all the stock the public does not buy, and in this way the salesman insures the sale of the goods, leaving nothing to chance. The conditions referred to are generally that the underwriters guarantee the sale of the stock at a specially low price. The stock is offered to the public at a higher price, more nearly representing its true value. Should the public buy all the stock the underwriters receive the difference between the specially low price and the price which the public paid for the goods. If the public do not buy readily, the underwriters themselves are compelled to buy at the low price agreed upon. The advantages of underwriting are thus perfectly obvious.

The gains arising out of incorporating the enterprise are several: (1) exemption from liability—the holders of stock are not liable for more than the amount of their holding should the company fail; (2) there is permanency, since the death of a stockholder does not affect the existence of the corporation, whereas in partnership it might lead to dissolution; (3) stockholders can sell their holdings to other people and invest elsewhere; (4) the officers are elected by vote, thus securing competent management; and (5) additional capital is more readily secured than in any other form of business organization.

It would be impossible in a brief lesson to describe all the ins and outs of a promotion scheme: the need of financing only sound businesses and how such businesses are tested; the certifying of the accounts; the staff changes due to reconstruction; and the promise of an increase in output and net receipts. These technical matters must be reserved for later study: our subject here is salesmanship and we have confined our attention strictly to that viewpoint.

EXERCISES

A. QUESTIONS FOR REVIEW:
   (1) Give a definition of promotion and show in what sense the promoter is a salesman.
   (2) What are the three requisites of a promotion?
   (3) Describe a promoter at work.

B. QUESTIONS FOR WRITTEN ANSWERS:
  (1) What is a promoter's greatest asset? And why?
  (2) Harry L. Henson is a man of wealth and good reputation who desires to form a company to run a light railway through a new region. George Parsons is a store dealer in a distant state who has a similar project for a region close at hand. Compare their advantages in promoting such enterprises.

(See Lesson XVI in the Sheldon Course of Business Building by Francis Cooper, author of "Financing an Enterprise.")

LESSON THIRTY-EIGHT
IN BUSINESS FOR YOURSELF

THE question as whether you intend to be in business on your own account, is important for two reasons: first, because some men do better as employés of a large corporation than they do as their own masters, therefore the decision calls for serious reflection: second, because no man can become a master without careful preparation, which should be begun as early as possible. He is in actual fact his own promoter—that is why I deal with the subject in this connection.

These are the days of enterprises with huge capital, and high grade employés have opportunities for earning salaries that in other days would have been impossible. The time will come when you arrive at the parting of the roads: one leads to a good post in the large corporation, and one leads to a business of your own. Which turning will you take? The answer to that question is not to be decided by mere feeling or desire. To want to have a business of your own is not sufficient proof that you could succeed, although every man who does succeed possesses this great desire to control his own affairs. Money is one of the primary necessities of the opening out of new enterprises, and money matters should always be viewed in the light of reason, rather than emotion. Again, there are some good men who are *essentially* employés—they are a great success as such, and as great a failure when they launch out on their own account. Are you one of these? I am not counselling you to take one road and not the other: I am simply telling you the facts. There are many retailers who earn much less than some of the commercial travellers who call upon them, and they carry a greater weight of care in addition.

Being in business for yourself is not necessarily the more profitable course, although it has its own compensations. And yet it may lead to a fortune beside which the salary of even a first class position may seem paltry.

But whichever turning you take there is one thing certain: you need ability, reliability, endurance and action. Let us suppose you have made up your mind to own, eventually, a retail store.

Enter the stock room of a large business and work your way up. Go through all the stages which will qualify you for travelling, and get the confidence of the firm. Travelling itself will give you a broader vision and incidentally imparts a vast amount of solid information about good locations for starting a business. In any event your journeys will educate you for future advancement, either by securing a more important position, or by enabling you to become your own master. Some firms indeed have been known to finance, in part, a trusted traveller who decides to take this step, giving him the opportunity of buying the stock they held until the new business became entirely his own. He may have provided the rest of the capital himself, or possibly he influenced others to put up the money. This leads me to point out the advisability of making plans in good time. Confidence is the basis of trade, and you will have to create this confidence by ability and character. Further, you must make business friends. This is to their advantage as well as to yours. They serve you eventually and you serve them. Apart from social fellowship, a desirable end in itself, there is the benefit of a mutual interchange of money and service.

But to attain this end you need a good plan, and a course of conduct in harmony with it. Know what you are going to do, and begin to do it. You then belong, not to the mentally blind, but to those who see. The future goal is in the distance, but every day it comes a little nearer, for your powers are being observed by other men and you are building up a reputation. You are selling your services now, and, when the time comes to sell your qualifications for mastership, the men who have money will doubtless be ready to stand by you by adding their dollars to those you have saved.

EXERCISE

Object Lesson. A good retail salesman from one of the local stores should be invited to give a selling talk to the class, offering goods about which the students are likely to know something. After the talk, questions can be asked or reasonable objections offered as to price or quality. When the salesman has been thanked for his services and has taken his departure, valuations of the talk, written or oral can be given. The tutor should conclude the lesson with a summing up.

G
WRITTEN SALESMANSHIP

LESSON THIRTY-NINE
THE THEORY OF WRITTEN SALESMANSHIP

SELLING goods by letter is not essentially different from salesmanship by personal appeal and argument; for every true sale, no matter by what means it is accomplished, obeys the same laws and fulfills the same end. A commercial traveller and an office salesman appeal to the same laws of human nature and they aim at the same finale—the satisfaction of the customer. But there are nevertheless several surface differences, and I wish to talk about these for a little while, as they form the theory of written salesmanship.

The outside man, going from city to city, is able to change his methods of approaching men and adapt them to the varying types of persons he meets. Smith, the grocer, is a smiling individual who likes to see everybody else smiling; but Brown, the hardware dealer, is gruff and prefers seriousness of demeanor in a salesman's methods. It is never wise to approach Robinson just before dinner when he is hungry and irritable, and Wilkins is always in good form about the time his dividend checks come in from property investments. Hence the man with the samples learns the arts of diplomacy and becomes a master in speaking in the right way, to the right person, at the right time.

It is very different with the office salesman. He cannot see, (and as a rule he does not know) the people to whom he writes. Before him are two lists of names and addresses: the first is that of persons to whom he is going to write, introducing an attractive line of goods; the second is that of persons who have replied to his advertisements. Of the first list he knows absolutely nothing. Their characters, their personal appearance, their likes and dislikes are a closed book. Of the second list he knows a little more. They are either curious or interested, otherwise they would not have answered the advertisement; their handwriting tells the story of education or the lack of it; their notepaper and residence may suggest wealth, moderate means or comparative poverty.

Even so, the office salesman has not as much knowledge of his customers as he would like to have, and therefore he conducts his operations on another basis altogether. He uses those fundamental needs and desires of our nature that are common to humanity the world over. A man may be of a smiling or a gruff disposition; he may be irritable before dinner and in good humor when his dividend checks arrive; he may be optimistic in stocking his store or just as niggardly; but whatever his characteristics he needs food to eat, clothes to wear, a house to live in, and certain little luxuries to make life happy.

Now, the office salesman addresses himself mainly to those needs and desires which are independent of personal peculiarities; he knows there are kinds of goods that men and women are either compelled to buy or will desire to buy, and therefore such goods do not require the personal appeal of a skilled salesman. He also knows that, whereas the travelling man can only call on a limited number of buyers weekly, the number that can be reached through the mails is ten times larger, and out of this larger number a volume of business can be completed which is as surprising as it is profitable.

In this way the mail order department overcomes the difficulty of a lack of knowledge of those whom it addresses. The task, however, is not easy. A profound acquaintance with human nature is needed, as well as success in all that pertains to office efficiency. To produce an impression in a 300-word letter, which an outside salesman could not produce without using 2,500, calls for skill of no mean order, and is often paid for at a salary of $125.00 a week. To divine the best way of dealing with the various requests and unfair demands of many correspondents, and to turn them into satisfactory sales, requires fine temper, literary ability and considerable experience.

The theory of written salesmanship is therefore founded in two facts: (a) the appeal to human needs which clamor for satisfaction, and (b) the possibility of reaching 10,000 people where the travelling salesman can reach only 1,00. The man who can turn this theory into good practice holds a fortune in his pen. A fine letter writer is highly valued in any sphere, be it social, literary or political; but in business he has a utilitarian value which, rendered in dollars, makes the selling letter an achievement worth seeking.

The lessons which are to follow, therefore, do not dwell upon fancies and notions about grammar and composition for their own sake; they tell you why poor English yields poor money, and how to write the other kind of English which yields dividends that would surprise the successful novelist.

EXERCISES

A. QUESTIONS FOR REVIEW:
   (1) Compare salesmanship by letter with the salesmanship of a commercial traveller.
   (2) To whom does the office salesman address himself?
   (3) State the two facts on which the theory of office salesmanship is based.

B. QUESTIONS FOR WRITTEN ANSWERS:
   (1) How does an office salesman overcome his lack of personal acquaintance with his correspondents?
   (2) What qualities are necessary in the office salesman and in his correspondence?

LESSON FORTY

What is a Selling Letter?

WHEN you sit down to write a business letter to another man, or to a group of men and women, your aim is so to word it that he, or they, will buy your goods and pay for them. A selling letter has therefore three qualities:

(1) It is a skillful arrangement of good arguments.
(2) Expressed in good English, about
(3) Good goods.

The goods must be good: of that there can be no doubt. Money has been made by fake schemes but only long enough to allow the news to get out. Years ago a man advertised a method of killing the famous potato bugs at twenty-five cents. Thousands paid their quarters and in return got a letter saying, "Take a block of wood and put the beetle on it; then take another block and put it on the bug. Squeeze the blocks together and kill the bug." Soon, however, the newspapers exposed the fake and the man decamped with the proceeds of his swindle. I do not suppose any sane man would be so foolish as to repeat this process nowadays with the boll weevil as a subject, but the principle is the same in offering any kind of goods that are not what they are represented to be. It is sheer madness to deceive the public if you want to succeed by gaining their confidence. You may use every device of literary art, and cunningly construct all kinds of plausible arguments so as to effect sales, but, if the goods on arrival are received with disappointment and anger, you are spending your money and energies to no purpose.

Nevertheless, good English and sound logic are necessary elements in the make-up of a selling letter. There is as much art in commercial composition as in the composition of a poem; and as much reasoning as in a lawyer's brief. By good English I mean not only correct grammar and punctuation, but the use of words in a manner that compels the reader to picture himself mentally in possession of the goods offered him because of the attractive method in which the letter describes them.

Ability to attain this end implies the power of literary description, the seizing of the salient points of an article and setting them forth in a few well-chosen phrases. To write good letters you must make your correspondents *see* the goods, and see themselves buying them. This power of creating mental visions resides to a large extent in the clever use of language.

But you must be a reasoner, also. The arguments should be strong, varied and conclusive. A few of them may be stronger than the others, and you will have to decide the order in which they are to be arranged. Sometimes there is one over-powering reason why the public should buy your goods, and you may find it advantageous to put that reason first, supporting it by the addition of auxiliary reasons later on. At other times you may feel that the article has three arguments in its favor, each of which is of the same weight, and you therefore select the one which offers the best material for a striking beginning. But, since a selling letter is a list, long or short, of reasons why the buyer should buy, it is evident these reasons must be as carefully sought out as they are cogently expressed in good English.

Business correspondence includes two other kinds of letters; that is, letters of complaint and letters asking for payment of accounts. Indirectly these, too, are selling letters, for if you answer the first indiscreetly, and write the second insolently, you are spoiling the market for future sales. Every office salesman has to write, or superintend the writing of such letters, and as the work is a matter of tact and experience, a lesson will be devoted to each kind of communication.

The three points mentioned at the beginning of the lesson are so brief as to be easily memorized; and, when you have written a letter, test it by using the three points as if they were three questions:

(1) Are the goods *good?*
(2) Is the English *good* English?
(3) Are the arguments both *good* and *skillfully arranged?*

EXERCISES

A. QUESTIONS FOR REVIEW:
 (1) What are the three qualities of a selling letter?
 (2) What is the argument against fake goods?
 (3) Why should the arguments be arranged in a prescribed order and expressed in good English?

B. QUESTIONS FOR WRITTEN ANSWERS:
 (1) How would you define a selling argument?
 (2) What is the special function of language in the composing of a selling letter?

LESSON FORTY-ONE
THE ARGUMENTS AND HOW TO ARRANGE THEM

AS previously stated, the arguments of a good selling letter are the reasons why a buyer should buy your goods. The task before you, therefore, is first to find out what those reasons are, and then to arrange them in the best way to effect a speedy sale, satisfactory to both parties.

Let us suppose you have a new fountain pen to dispose of, one that claims to overcome all the little eccentricities of the articles, good, bad and indifferent, that now flood the market. You take a sheet of paper and in reply to the question, "Why do I think a man ought to buy this pen?" you write down one, two, three, perhaps six good reasons. Some of them may be more important than others, but that point can be dealt with later. When finished, your list of arguments would be something like this:

1. The pen is cheap in price and simple in construction.
2. It solves the "flow of ink" problem by a new patent regulator.
3. It is very light, being made of a quite new material.
4. The mechanism for re-filling is also a patent and prevents inky fingers.
5. Leaking is impossible and the pen may safely be carried upside down.
6. It was successfully tried by six men, an accountant, a professor, a commercial traveller, a grocer, a butcher, and a farmer, for one year before being put on the market.

Probably other reasons could be produced for an early purchase, but these will be needed for follow-up letters.

The question now arises: "Which argument should come first? and second? and third? What principle of order should be followed?" The answer is, "Follow the mental law of sale." Every buyer's mind passes, more or less quickly, through well defined stages of thought and feeling in making a purchase, and therefore

it is your duty and advantage to adapt your argument to the law governing those stages. They are:
1. Favorable attention.
2. Interest.
3. Desire.
4. Decision and Action.

Consequently the argument that offers the best material as an attention getter is the argument to be put first. Now look at your list. No. 1 will not do because there are plenty of cheap fountain pens. No. 2 is better, but No. 3 is on the same level as No. 1, there being scores of light pens to be had at any store. No. 4 is promising, and so is No. 5. No. 6 is a reason supplementary to the argument of the other five. Your choice then is between No. 2, No. 4 and No. 5, and you will notice each has to do with the containing and the flowing of the ink. Do fountain pens usually give most trouble in the stoppage of the flow, or in the re-filling, or in leaking into the pocket? If you have not used one for any length of time you can get the opinion of others who have. I think you will find that the leaking and the re-filling troubles are confined to very cheap pens, whilst stoppages in the flow sometimes afflict even the very best pens. Therefore, as your pen is fitted with a perfect regulator it will be wise to seize this fact and use it as an attention getter. Cheapness and lightness have no attention-attracting materials in them, for the chances are your correspondent may be using a pen embodying these qualities and yet giving no satisfaction; but if your first sentence tells him about one which solves an inconvenient problem, he is likely to read on, though he may be a little skeptical.

You have, however, got his attention, and you bolster up your case by referring to the testimony of the men who have given the pen twelve months' trial. He probably knows one or two of them by repute and begins to think the article may be a success. He is now interested in the proposition. By this time you have used points No. 2 and No. 6, and you strengthen your contention by proceeding to outline No. 4 and No. 5.

After that, the application of the selling arguments is begun. You show that the fountain pen, so admittedly wonderful, is simple in construction, very light and cheap. By this time the reader's interest has changed into desire and desire into decision. "Here," he says, "is a pen as cheap as any other pen but infinitely superior. Why should I not buy one?" He fills in the order form, encloses the remittance, and you have made a sale.

But if you had begun your letter by writing a long paragraph on the cheapness of the pen, or even the new and light material of which the body of it is made, you might not, probably would not, have secured the attention you did. Your letter, failing to arrest attention at the outset, would have dropped into the waste basket. You see why it is not only necessary to have good arguments but to know how to use them.

I will now take two letters dealing with a matter quite different from fountain pens, namely, the selling of advertising space. The A letter has good arguments unskillfully arranged; the B letter corrects this fault.

A

Chicago, Feb. 10th, 1905.

Mr. John Thompson,
   138 Canal Street, Chicago, Ill.
Dear Sir:

We want to submit for your careful consideration, some of the principal reasons why you should advertise in our publication, *The Kansas Corn Grower.*

The first reason lies in the fact that this publication, now in its fifth year, has a larger circulation among the prosperous farmers of Kansas than any other monthly publication in this State.

The second reason why you should advertise with us is, because, from the outset, *The Kansas Corn Grower* has been ably edited, and its advertising columns have been clean, so that our readers are not suspicious regarding the advertisements which appear therein, but are ready to accept as true just what you say about the goods you advertise.

The third reason we want to mention is that farmers in the State of Kansas have plenty of money to spend just at this time, owing to the fact that the corn crop has been large in Kansas during the past two years and prices have been good. As a consequence, the farmers have more money to spend than ever before in the history of the State. According to State Reports recently compiled, the average income of Kansas Farmers for 1904 was $1,050.00 over and above what they consumed.

The fourth reason we want to mention is that our rates—only 15c per line—for a circulation, guaranteed, of 33,840, is so low that you can well afford to advertise in the columns of *The Kansas Corn Grower.*

It pays others; it will pay you. Kindly let us hear from you on the subject if you are interested. Write for a copy of the paper and any information you would like to have.

Excuse this long letter, but we want to lay the matter before you in an intelligent way.

Please let us hear from you by return mail, and much oblige,

Yours respectfully,
THE KANSAS CORN GROWER,
Kernel & Cobb, Publishers.
Chicago, Feb. 10, 1905.

B

Mr. John Thompson,
138 Canal St., Chicago, Ill.

Dear Sir:

Here is something that will interest you.

Out here in Kansas, the farmers are unusually prosperous just now. This is shown by a report just issued by the State Department of Agriculture, crediting the farmers of the state with an average income of $1,050.00 for 1904.

A total for the farmers of the state of $75,348,000.

This means that one-half of that amount, or $37,674,000, will be spent during the next six months. Are you interested in knowing how to get a good share of this trade? Here is our suggestion.

Thirty-three thousand of the most prosperous farmers in this prosperous state pay for, read and farm by *The Kansas Corn Grower*. The income of these 33,000 farmers will easily average one-third more than the average farmer, as they comprise the intelligent and most prosperous class.

The aggregate spending money of our 33,000 subscribers for the next six months amounts to about $23,000,000. You can get your share of this trade at small outlay. Here's our plan—a splendid one for you, and a good one for us.

Buy from us, 160 lines per month in the next six issues of *The Kansas Corn Grower*. The cost to you will be only $135.00, or about 40c per subscriber for six months' advertising.

This advertisement will be adequate in size—about 5¼ inches double column—to give you a sure-to-be-seen advertisement. Make the advertisement right and it will be the best advertising investment you ever made.

If you cannot get up the right kind of copy, submit your proposition to us and we will put it in shape for you. We will get up a series of six advertisements if you wish us to do so. We advise a change of copy in most instances.

We are confident that we can make the use of liberal space pay you.

We are sending you a copy of our publication by even mail, and enclose herewith order blank and printed matter containing testimonials, etc.

THE ART OF SELLING

This is a straight business proposition that will, we are sure, appeal to you if you want Kansas trade.

Yours for more business,
KERNEL & COBB,
Publishers *The Kansas Corn Grower*.

These letters are reproduced by permission of H. M. Van Hoesen Company from "Letters," Vol. I, May, 1905.

EXERCISES

A. QUESTIONS FOR REVIEW:
  (1) State the first object of a selling letter writer.
  (2) What is the law regulating the order of the arguments?
  (3) Why would it be a mistake to refer to the cheapness of the new fountain pen in the first paragraph of the letter?

B. QUESTIONS FOR WRITTEN ANSWERS:
  (1) How is the letter B an improvement on A in the order of its arguments?
  (2) The following reasons for purchasing a new desk dictionary of English words are to be arranged in their true order.
   1. It is handy in size.
   2. It is the result of a careful study of social, commermercial and literary correspondence.
   3. It is designed for home and office use.
   4. It is cheap.
   5. It contains 25,000 words.
   6. You can find what you want in a moment.
   7. Has a list of synonyms and prepositions used with verbs.
   8. Supplied with tags.

LESSON FORTY-TWO

Effective English

IN this lesson I shall treat of the use of words as a means of expressing selling ideas; and a selling idea is an argument why the buyer should buy.

At the outset it is well to remember that the great majority of buyers are not critics of language on the lookout for mistakes in grammar and composition, or for beautiful ideas beautifully expressed. They are plain folks who, when they open your letter, want to know what it is all about, and it is up to you to get their attention, arouse their desire, and effect a sale. To touch their literary sensibilities by lofty sentiments in finely chiselled phrases is no part of your business. When they have finished reading the letter, you do not want them to say, "A most charming composition." You want them to say, "I'm going to BUY that cream jug," or whatever the article may be. Your object is not to display your power as a master of phrases but to draw attention to your goods. And yet it is just this mastery of phrases that brings business by letter writing, hence the importance of devoting a lesson to the study of the subject.

The power that is greatest in the writing of selling letters, from the literary point of view, is that of *personality*. I will try to show you what I mean. Think of half a dozen men you know. When you have their names in mind, think of the differences that mark them off one from another. Perhaps there are no special differences—yes, you think of one man who always seems to express himself in a manner all his own; he has what is called a "way" with him that is nobody else's way. When he talks you say "it is just like him." Now most people talk just like other people. They are copyists. But this man has his own way; he is "different;" in short he has personality.

It is the same in letter writing. Scores of office salesmen write like other office salesmen, but here and there you find one who has "a way of his own." Compare his letters with the letters of other men and you feel they are "different;" he writes with *personality*.

Can this desirable quality be cultivated? Certainly. But do not run away with the notion that a short term of apprenticeship will bring you to the level of the man I have just described. You may never quite attain that level, but study and right methods will give you a position a long way above the average.

The first duty is to resolve not to be a copyist. Read model letters by all means, and when you have absorbed the spirit of them as distinct from the phraseology, *forget* them. Look at your goods with your own eyes and then think of them in relation to the world of buyers. Get selling points that are not obvious to everybody, and find out ways of expressing those points that are new and striking. This means *thought,* but there is no success nowadays without it—indeed there never has been.

Mr. W. D. Moody says, "Six men relate the same funny story; only one, however, tells it with point. On the same principle, six men might tell the story of a typewriter, and only one make the point clear and strong." That *one* is the man who individualized the story by thinking of it until it gathered strength and character from this mental industry.

Effective English, therefore, is not primarily a knowledge of nouns, verbs and adjectives: these are its technical constituents no doubt, but the force of a selling letter, considered as a literary product, is its personality; and this arises out of the soul of the writer himself—his mind diligently applied to the portrayal of the goods in relation to the needs of the public, language being the medium of expression.

There are certain rules of a technical kind the observance of which contributes to the writing of effective English. The first is *avoid hackneyed expressions* such as "your favor to hand," "esteemed order," "valued support," and "assuring you of our best attention." Anything that tends to make a letter commonplace and conventional should be taboo. I do not say there are no conventions in business correspondence: you acknowledge receipt of a check, or advise a consignee of the dispatch of goods in the boldest of phrases, and it is right to do so. The recipients do not want anything else. But in composing selling letters you have a different viewpoint, and as your first aim is to get attention, you cannot afford to begin by hoping to receive the reader's "esteemed" something or other. The nerve path in his brain goes straight as an arrow from the word "esteemed" to the word "waste-basket."

The second rule is that *your meaning must be clear*. Usually letter writers err on the side of length: they use too many words in the effort to make themselves understood. Concise phraseology is necessary to a clear meaning, and equally necessary to economize the time of the reader. He will not sit down to read a letter that looks like an essay: he either refuses to read a word of it, or he puts it on one side and forgets it, which amounts to the same thing. Condensation is an art that should be learned early, and the best way to begin is to select a model letter and say all it contains in half the number of words, and say it with more clearness and emphasis.

The third rule is to *acquire a knowledge of words in themselves* and of *their commercial uses in combination*. Illustrations of a literary kind are plentiful. Take this one:

> A violet by a mossy stone.

The words are simple enough, but their combination results in a beautiful picture. Observe the *color* suggestions: there is the violet flower; the green moss; and the grey stone: a most delicate nature miniature in six words.

Now the same principle has its uses in commercial correspondence. Selling letters are not composed anyhow: the writer carefully *selects* his words and just as carefully arranges them with a view to making a picture, to wit, the picture of his goods and the buyer as already enjoying the possession of them. Here is a phrase from an advertisement:

> "Don't *envy* a good complexion. Use massage cream and *have* one."

Notice how skillfully the writer has used eleven words to tell and to enforce his story. Can you not see the picture of a whole host of people admiring a woman, the delicate tint of whose coloring arouses envy in the eyes of the beholders? Five words suffice to create that picture, and the next six words form the selling talk that shows how *envy* may be transmuted into *possession*.

This is a sample of effective English from the language viewpoint, and in composing letters I should like you to realize that time consumed in the preparation of a single sentence, or even on the mere order of words, is not time wasted but time invested. You have to get attention, arouse desire and secure action; and to succeed demands an increasing amount of skill.

By taking a serious view of what is required you will avoid the anyhow system of writing letters. The boy at school who has to write a class composition often does it in the school spirit, which is "I *have* to go through with it and the sooner the better." When he is older and applies for a position, he takes immense pains with his letter of application, for much depends on the issue. This is the spirit of the true office salesman: he takes immense pains with his letters for much depends on the issue.

EXERCISES

A. QUESTIONS FOR REVIEW:
  (1) What power is the greatest in the writing of selling letters? Why?
  (2) State three technical rules that contribute to effective English.
  (3) How much does the letter writer owe to the selection and arrangement of words?

B. QUESTIONS FOR WRITTEN ANSWERS:
  (1) Is a business letter, composed in exquisite English, necessarily a good selling letter? Give reasons for your answer.
  (2) "You can picture your goods by using a photograph or colored illustration; therefore effective English is not necessary to a good selling letter." Answer this objection.

LESSON FORTY-THREE
ON ANSWERING INQUIRIES

WHEN a correspondent addresses an inquiry to you or your firm he is obviously in need of information which it is your duty to communicate to him in a letter that he can understand. It may also be your duty to do more than that, for in no part of business correspondence is there so much room for initiative and judgment as in the answering of inquiries. Occasionally the inquiry itself will be so vague that it is almost impossible to know what the writer means. You may get a letter like this:

"Gentlemen:
   Please send me some of that stuff which the children sometimes eat, it is a long brownish thing with hard seeds in it and sweet. They told me the name of it but I have forgotten what they said. You will know the kind of stuff I mean. I enclose $1.00, and should think 3 lbs. of it would be enough.
                             Yours truly,
                                  Ben. D. Blossom."

Now you *might* write a sharp letter to Mr. Blossom in reply, telling him if he would be good enough to say what he really *did* want you would try to oblige him, but that, as written, his letter is double Dutch. Mr. Blossom would reply in similar strain, saying it was clear you did not know your business and would you be good enough to return his money.

The better plan is to put the original letter before you, and, if "locust bean" does not occur to you at once, *think* until it does. You are an office salesman in order to serve your employers and the public, and you do *not* serve them by making Mr. Blossom feel uncomfortable. So send him his locust beans with the change out of his remittance; and when he meets a friend who wants something of which he has forgotten the name he is sure to say, "Write to Bolt & Co. *They'll* get it for you." *Service* is the secret of success.

Another type of vague letter is that where the responsibility of choosing an article is placed upon the salesman:

"Gentlemen:

I enclose $4.00. I want a small wedding present for a friend but do not know what to choose. Can you suggest something? I don't want a salt cellar, as the parties have three already, as well as two 'Lives of Lincoln.' I do hope you can suggest something as you know so many things.

Yours truly,
(Miss) Molly Davies."

"P. S.—I have just heard they have a quilt with a star and stripes pattern, so don't send one of them."

It would be very easy for you to poke fun at Miss Davies in a letter saying that not much could be bought for $4.00; and possibly you want to give your best attention to the big orders for suites of furniture, or expensive jewelry, leaving small orders and inquiries until the end of the day, when, being weary, you simply ask for a more definite order.

The right course is mentally to run over the four dollar articles, mark some of them in the catalogue, or enumerate them in a letter, and then ask Miss Davies which she prefers. You can please her better that way than by selecting an article haphazard and dispatching it.

I have had nothing to say hitherto about letters of inquiry that are straightforward, simply because they offer no special problems for consideration. All they require is the information asked for, and yet there is an art in doing this effectively. For instance, here is an inquiry and two letters in reply, one of them bad, the other good:

Gentlemen:

A friend of mine took me to a house the other night where I saw a lovely picture that seized my fancy immediately. It represents a mediaeval scene, where some women are raising a coffin lid in a subterranean chamber, disclosing a face with wonderfully fine features. There are roses on the floor. I think I have seen the picture before somewhere, but there was no name on this one, and my friend could not tell me what it was. I had no opportunity to ask my host—indeed, I did not care to show my ignorance.

From the description given can you identify the picture? If so, how much is a copy framed and unframed?

Yours truly,
Ira M. Burt.

You see at once he is referring to Rossetti's "Dante's Dream." This is the short, sharp, and—bad method of replying to such an inquiry:

Dear Sir:

The picture you refer to in yours of ———— is the well known Rossetti's "Dante's Dream." Unframed in colors it is $10.00, 14x21"; in engraving $3.00. Framing would cost you $3.00, black and gold, with mount.   Yours truly,

Bolt & Co.

This letter gives the information, but it "gives" it by *throwing* it at the inquirer.

Here is a better style:

Dear Sir:

We are very glad to be of service to you in identifying the picture you saw in a friend's house. It is Rossetti's "Dante's Dream," and the colored reproduction (14x21") which we sell, framed in black and gold, for $13.00, is a delight to the artistic sense, and calculated to adorn the walls of your drawing room. Unframed, the cost is reduced by $3.00. We have also an engraving of the picture at $3.00, the same size as the other and costing the same amount to frame. It is excellent value at the price but of course lacks the warmth of the original colors.

It will afford us pleasure to receive your order for one of these reproductions.   Yours truly,

Bolt & Co.

Now compare these two answers. The first is too short; it does not contain sufficient *expansion* of the information which Mr. Burt is anxiously expecting, and the tone is curt: there is no humanity in it; it does not sympathize with the finder's joy in the picture, a copy of which he is eager to buy. Further, the letter contains a subtle insult. It rebuffs Mr. Burt for his ignorance by telling him the picture is "well known," thus accentuating a feeling already too intense.

The second letter is cheery and human throughout. It, so to speak, shakes hands with Mr. Burt and rejoices with him in his "find," instead of icily informing him the picture is "well known.' Moreover, it makes the facts and figures read like a talk instead of like a catalogue, as in the first letter, and it gives him a better idea of the difference between the two reproductions.

So take pains with inquiry letters. Give answers that make your correspondents feel you want to help them and serve them, and the best way to do that is to cultivate the spirit of service.

EXERCISES

A. QUESTIONS FOR REVIEW:
   (1) What is the salesman's duty in dealing with rather obscure inquiries?
   (2) How would you answer a letter containing a request that you choose an article for the writer?
   (3) What word ought to be kept in mind as a guiding principle in answering inquiries?

B. QUESTIONS FOR WRITTEN ANSWERS:
   (1) Why is the second letter from Bolt & Company an improvement on the first, as a *selling* letter?
   (2) Write a reply to the following inquiry:

Bolt & Co.,
   Memphis, Tenn.
Gentlemen:
   Can you tell me who is the author of the book called "Tom Brown's School Days"? Me and another fellow had a long argument about it. He said the author was Tom Brown himself, and I said he was called Hews.
   If I am right I want to buy a copy to prove he is wrong. Reply soon.
                         Yours truly,
                                Bill Johnson.

LESSON FORTY-FOUR

LETTERS OF COMPLAINT AND HOW TO ANSWER THEM

THERE are three possible sources of trouble in delivering goods that have been ordered by mail. They are delays (a) in the mail itself, (b) in the firm's dispatch, and (c) in the railroad or other form of freight. The office salesman receives a letter like this:

9 Englewood St.,
Croydon, Wis.,
Jan. 7, 1910.

The Battle Store,
   Sioux City, Ia.
Gentlemen:
   On the 1st inst. I ordered a specially bound copy of "Uncle Tom's Cabin" at $1.50 as quoted in your catalogue, but up to the present I have not had either a reply or the book. This is the second time I have had trouble with your firm and if it occurs again I shall transfer my dealings elsewhere.
Yours truly,
John S. Dickinson.

Inquiry is made at once, but no entry can be found to show that the first letter has been received. Just as a reply to this effect is about to be dictated, the postman brings the missing letter. It had been directed in mistake to Sioux Falls by Mr. Dickinson and the delay therefore arose out of his own carelessness. The book is promptly packed and sent off. The salesman dictates a letter explaining the cause of the delay, and enclosing the incriminating envelope as witness. He adds at the close these words: "If you would exercise a little more charity in judging other people you would spare yourself a good deal of worry and save us a lot of extra trouble."

Now that is a fatal blunder, for although it may be quite true it is not expedient to say so. A wise salesman would write a letter like this:

THE ART OF SELLING

The Battle Store,
Sioux City,
Jan. 9, 1910.

Mr. John S. Dickinson,
9 Englewood St.,
Croydon, Wis.

Dear Sir:

On receipt of your letter of the 7th we immediately made a search for yours of the 1st, as we could not understand why any order with which you favored us had not been filled. Whilst the search was being made, the missing letter was brought by the postman, having been delayed on account of an incorrect address—see envelope herewith.

Please find receipt attached for $1.50 with our thanks. The book was dispatched by an early mail today and we feel sure you will be satisfied with its type, illustrations and binding.

The enclosed circular describing the new Life of Mrs. Harriet Beecher Stowe will no doubt interest you, and we should be glad to have you fill in the order form for a copy to be sent to you on the date of publication.

Yours sincerely,
The Battle Store,
J. G.

It is easy to see how far the wise man's letter is in advance of that written by the first salesman. So soon as Mr. Dickinson sees the envelope he himself had wrongly addressed, he knows he has written the Battle Store a most impolite letter of complaint; but imagine the difference between the feelings aroused by the two answers. If he got the first salesman's letter he would in his heart of hearts feel that he had acted rashly, and had given the store a lot of unnecessary trouble. For that reason he would be inclined not to trouble them again. But if he got the second letter, charged as it is with a courteous and businesslike spirit throughout, he would feel a subtle sense of indebtedness to the firm because it had refused to take advantage of his slip of the pen by writing a sharp epistle in return. He would say, "These people are worth encouraging;" and in all likelihood he would fill in the order form for a copy of the new book.

The difference between the two salesmen is that one believes in the tit for tat policy and loses a customer; the other believes in the good for evil policy and retains a customer. And a salesman who turns a customer's wrath into more dollars is a salesman *par excellence.*

Delays that arise through the incompetence of the staff are not so easily dealt with. You cannot answer a letter of complaint arising out of carelessness on the premises by simply admitting the fault, much less by telling untruths as to the retribution meted out to the offender.

There is a story told of a manager who answered a complaining letter by saying he had dismissed the bookkeeper at a moment's notice. He had done nothing of the kind, and when the writer of the complaining letter called at the office for the bookkeeper's name and address (in order to find him a new job) the manager was in a tight corner and had to invent a brand new lie to get out of the old one.

There ought to be a good reason for every defect in the handling of orders, and therefore a satisfactory explanation for every complaint that follows. A fire in the stock room is a plea which every disappointed customer can understand, but a sudden shortage in the supply of brown paper had better remain unconfessed. Efficiency all day and every day is the only law, and the best way of answering letters of complaint is to make them impossible.

Few things make a customer more angry than to have letters and printed matter sent to his old address after he has mailed in a notice of removal. And yet I have known cases where a firm has promised "not to do it again" on two occasions, and has sinned for the third time, one address book, not often used, having been forgotten in the previous alterations. Such instances are doubtless unusual, but they only prove the need of a perfect office machine.

Where complaints arise from the nature of the goods, the only policy to pursue is to return the money and get the goods back again. To compel acceptance because "an order is an order," is not to serve the public. The goods may be all you say they are, but if the buyer is dissatisfied why foist them upon him? He will never buy at your store again if he can avoid it.

In answering letters of complaint due to the delay or damage of goods in the course of transit by rail or by water, the office salesman may cool his impatience by remembering that the angry customer will not put the blame on the firm that sells. Every buyer knows from experience what are the possibilities of a journey by rail and on the river. Still this is small comfort for both parties to the transaction, and as the seller is likely to suffer more than the buyer, it behooves him to master problems of transportation so that nothing is left undone to insure quick and safe delivery of goods.

The one sound rule in answering letters of complaint is "Be courteous." Never lose your temper. Explain, but do not argue. Seek to mollify the customer's wrath instead of feeding it by numerous contentions. The philosophy of the "soft answer" holds good today as it did thousands of years ago.

EXERCISES

A. QUESTIONS FOR REVIEW:
  (1) What are the three sources of trouble in delivering goods ordered by mail?
  (2) Would you answer a reviling letter in the same spirit? If not, why?
  (3) What is the surest method of handling complaints?

B. QUESTIONS FOR WRITTEN ANSWERS:
  (1) Give an illustration from your own experience of the power of the soft answer to turn away wrath. If you cannot remember one, explain the reason why a calm letter is more effective than an angry one.
  (2) Write a reply to the following complaint:

Bolt & Co.,
   Memphis, Tenn.
Gentlemen:

You have again sent a letter to my old address at 239 Black St., although I have before me your acknowledgment of my notification of the change. Do you want me to organize an office system for you so as to prevent these mistakes? If you do this again I shall cancel all my business for the future. The man who lives at 239 rang me up and was very impertinent about my correspondence being addressed there. He asked me if I thought I still owned the house. This must be stopped.

                        Yours truly,
                              Henry Drake.

LESSON FORTY-FIVE
FOLLOW-UP LETTERS

AN office salesman, knowing that in many instances his first letter to the people named on a list of prospective buyers will not be successful, writes a series of letters to "follow up" the first. The problem before him is to ascertain how many of these follow-up letters to write and to send out; and what to say in them.

Manifestly, he will, at the very beginning of the campaign, arrange the whole series from the first to the last. To spend all his ammunition in the first letter and have none for the others would be poor policy; hence he carefully investigates the list of selling arguments with a view to using some in the first letter and one or two in each of the "follow-ups."

No communication should leave the office without a definite mission to fulfil. If the first letter and the first follow-up have yielded no result, the second follow-up must deal with the matter from a different viewpoint.

Thus the office salesman is as much a strategist with the pen as the general is with the sword. The only danger lies in allowing a follow-up system to become a fixture. A system of repeated canvass by letter may appear very logical and quite convincing *on paper,* but if the results are unsatisfactory it is time to change it for something newer. Business systems are like Christian morals: they are governed by a law which says, "By their fruits ye shall know them." So beware of fine follow-up devices, with all their elaborate methods and accompanying circulars, but which accomplish little or nothing. The true system is found in adaptation to changing circumstances—the adaptation seen in *results.*

Naturally the form and contents of follow-up letters will vary according to the kind of business. A correspondence college will not employ the same methods as a dry goods store; and the number of letters sent is also determined largely by the same fact. But any number over five, sent at intervals of ten days, is usually inadvisable. If you cannot sell your goods to a man after five skilled applications by letter it is hardly likely you will succeed by any further solicitation. Doubtless there are cases where you will effect a sale by a sixth letter, for the receiver says, "Those people are so much in earnest I will accept their offer." But the number of such successes is not large enough to justify the expenditure.

On the other hand, you do not serve the interests of your firm by getting a reputation for "bombarding" people. Scores decide to accept or reject your goods after the receipt of the first follow up, and if you persist in writing to them again and again you render yourself liable to the charge of pestering people with unwelcome attentions. The law of averages, however, proves that until after the receipt of the fifth follow-up, a correspondent makes no demur; he accepts your communications as evidence of an earnest desire to sell, but he appears to think you should give him up after that as a "no prospect."

Follow-up letters are usually printed in imitation typewriting, or produced on an office machine in such a way as to convey the impression that they have been typewritten. The names and addresses are filled in by the stenographer, care being taken to use a ribbon with exactly the same color as that of the rest of the letter. Unless this part of the work is well done the recipient sees through the device. He knows that hundreds of other people are receiving the same letter, word for word, and that the writer wants them all to believe he is writing specially and personally to them as individuals. In this attempt he often signally fails, and it is a failure that does no good to the firm.

No doubt the difficulties are many. The cost of typing thousands of letters every week and the work of signing them by hand are items that few firms face with equanimity. They assert that the form letter, as previously described, is effective and that, even if the recipient detects the signs of its manufacture in the rubber stamp signature and the slightly different color of the ink in the address, he does not trouble about it.

That may be true in some cases, but the fact still remains—*personal* letters achieve more results than *form* letters. The question then arises: Can the office salesman afford to write personal letters, in the sense of having form letters typed on a machine? I do not think he can, at any rate in large businesses where the mailing list is a long one. The only course open to him, at any rate for the time being, is to put money into printing machine methods for producing letters so good that they cannot be distinguished from those which have been specially typed. Written signatures, or at least initials in ink are desirable, and close attention to the use of the ribbon in typing the addresses is obviously necessary. Carelessness in this detail means absolute failure. The impression you seek to convey is replaced by its direct opposite. What is worth doing at all is worth doing well.

It is my firm belief, however, that in the future the imitation typewritten form letter will be superseded by a kind of letter that does away with the necessity of trying to deceive, however innocently, the eye of the reader. It will be a *printed* form letter, but printed in such a way as to compel attention, and more care than ever will be exercised in its composition. The advantages of such a letter are easily seen. There is no need to disguise anything by imitating something else; you tell the same story in the same way to everybody; and the present complicated office arrangements for sending out form letters are replaced by a simple system.

The one fact, however, that will hasten this event is the growing inability of the public to distinguish between a form letter and one specially typewritten. You can imitate so perfectly that after a while you defeat your own ends; and when you find a *real* letter treated as a *form* letter it is time to make a change. The change may not come immediately but it is wise to prepare for it.

EXERCISES

A. QUESTIONS FOR REVIEW:
  (1) What is a follow up letter?
  (2) How many should be dispatched? What is the limit, and why?
  (3) State the arguments for and against letters in imitation typewriting.

B. QUESTIONS FOR WRITTEN ANSWERS:
  (1) "The end in view decides the means to be used." Comment on this so far as it refers to follow up letters.
  (2) What is the probable future of the *form* letter?

LESSON FORTY-SIX
SELLING YOUR SERVICES BY LETTER

THERE are several ways of securing a salaried position, and one of them is by answering an advertisement. More knowledge and skill are required in doing this than is commonly supposed; and if you had read fifty or a hundred applications from candidates for a vacancy you would fully realize the importance of good penmanship, correct grammar and punctuation, crisp style and condensed form.

Here is an advertisement from the Chicago Tribune:

"Young man for general office work; one who understands bookkeeping preferred; good opportunity for a hard and willing worker. Salary to start $10. Address W 338, Tribune."

Some young men would reply as follows:

Gentlemen:

I saw your advertisement and think I should suit you. I was six months in the office of Sharp & Co., Engineers, and have been three months with S. P. Marks & Co., in State St.

I know bookkeeping and have helped to keep a set of books. Am eighteen years of age. Testimonials good. They give me nine dollars where I am now.

Hoping to hear from you, I am,

Yours truly,

Thomas G. Binks.

Note the weak points of this letter.

(1) He does not say where he saw the advertisement and the advertiser probably wants to know, as he may be "keying" and otherwise testing his ads.

(2) He does not say what kind of office work he has done and is doing. Even his reference to bookkeeping is very indefinite—what does it mean to "know" bookkeeping?

(3) He writes as if he were telegraphing. "Am eighteen years of age. Testimonials good." *Write* your application; don't *jerk* it out.

(4) He shows no idea of composition. We get the notion of a youth who said, "H'm, I'll just answer this ad. *Might* get the

job. Might not. Dollar advance anyhow. What shall I say? (Seizes paper and dashes off a letter.) H'm. That'll do!"

The proper way to reply to the ad is as follows:

Gentlemen:

In offering myself as a candidate for the vacancy advertised in this morning's Tribune, I should like to say that I am eighteen years of age and have had one year's experience in the office of Wilson, Jones & Co., Importers, Michigan Avenue, first as stenographer, and then as assistant bookkeeper. I feel, however, that there is not much scope for advancement in the business, and as the salary is not adequate I am looking out for a bigger opportunity. If, as stated in your ad, there is room to grow in your establishment, I think I could make terms with you, as I don't mind hard work if the future holds some reward for it.

Before leaving my present position, however, I should like to be assured that it is worth my while to do so—the salary in both cases being identical. I can see you at your office any day between twelve and one p. m.

Yours truly,
Henry H. Ordemann.

Note the points of this letter.

(1) The writer has taken pains to express himself in clear English, the style being free and unconstrained.

(2) He goes to the real point, namely, that the firm wants a youth who is a hard worker. He proves his case by showing that what he will get is not an advance in salary but a bigger opportunity. That is the kind of man every sensible employer needs.

(3) He is dignified and independent. He will not accept the new position unless he is sure it offers greater scope for advancement. The chances are ten to one that nearly all the other applicants are toeing the line in the spirit of supplication. Here is a youth who says, politely, of course, that the position must be what he requires or he will not accept it. Such an attitude is calculated to beget confidence far more readily than that of the man who in a roundabout manner beseeches the advertiser, saying, "Do give *me* the job."

Mr. Binks and Mr. Ordemann, the two applicants in question, are salesmen. The former is a poor specimen; he does not know how to describe his goods,—that is, his services, to a possible buyer, —that is, the employer. He puts no brains and no earnestness into the work. The other man does both and will be rapidly advancing to fortune whilst Binks is at a standstill.

EXERCISES

A. QUESTIONS FOR REVIEW:
   (1) Enumerate the qualities of a good letter applying for a position.
   (2) What are the chief faults of poor letters of application?
   (3) In what sense is an applicant a salesman?

B. QUESTIONS FOR WRITTEN ANSWERS:
   (1) If the goods you offer to your prospective employer are your services, and the goods should be analyzed, how would you analyze your knowledge of shorthand and typewriting?
   (2) Answer the following advertisement:

There is a good opportunity for a stenographer (male) in a new business on the lake shore. Must be young and active, and accurate in work. Splendid opening for the right kind of youth. Apply giving full particulars and stating salary. Box 512 Tribune.

LESSON FORTY-SEVEN
COLLECTING ACCOUNTS

ALTHOUGH the majority of people are honest in their dealings, experience proves the advisability of instituting cash transactions wherever possible. "Money with order" is a sound principle for both buyer and seller.

But there are circumstances where credit becomes a necessity, or an advantage which creates a necessity, and out of this arises the occasional delays which call for (1) the letter of reminder, (2) the letter of expostulation, and (3) the letter which threatens penalties. Let us look at these.

John Avery has a monthly account with Bolt & Co. and fails to pay at the time appointed. You decide to send him a letter of reminder. How ought it to be phrased? That depends on his past character as a customer. If he is usually a good payer you deal very gently with him; if not, you add a word or two as to the delays that continue to mark his record. Supposing he is usually a good payer you write thus:

Dear Sir:

If, as is your custom, you promptly sent us a remittance on the 31st ult., it has not yet arrived and must have gone astray in the mails. We thought it best to advise you of the non-receipt.

Yours very truly,

Bolt & Co.

If he is getting a reputation for slackness you would say to him:

Dear Sir:

We regret to observe your account is again in arrears, although it should have been paid fourteen days ago. Had this been the first occasion on which we found it necessary to apply for payment we might have allowed the delay to pass longer, but as it is becoming periodic we wish to ask you in a quite friendly spirit to oblige us by being a little more prompt.

When our customers fail us in this way, limiting our funds for cash transactions in placing large orders, we cannot render them the good service we have done hitherto, and these delays tend to raise prices.

You will see therefore that the early settlement of account is for your own benefit.

Kindly send a remittance by return mail.

Yours truly,

Bolt & Co.

There are some men, however, who *can* pay and *won't;* some who *would* but *can't.* How are you to write to these when they reply to your letters of reminder and expostulation? The answer is that each case must be dealt with on its merits. In a sense you have been selling goods plus credit, and you do not want to lose both the goods and the cash. So remember that you are still a salesman even when writing dunning letters. It is delicate work, requiring sympathetic insight combined with a display of firmness.

Mrs. French keeps a small store in a country town and owes you $25.00 which amount was due on the 31st of January. It is now February 16, and you have had no reply to your expostulatory letter. This delay in payment has become chronic and you begin to question the wisdom of further credit. On the other hand, she has always paid eventually.

A letter arrives next morning. It says:

Gentlemen:

I received your letter but I am sorry I can't pay the $25.00 yet. I don't think I could pay even $10.00, for my daughter had to have an operation on her neck and it fairly cleaned me out. Surely a big store like yours does not need my few dollars and can wait a little longer for the money. Anyhow I can't pay it now, and that's all there is to it.

Yours truly,

Sarah J. French.

At first you regard this letter as a trifle impertinent, but, looking closer, you see signs that Mrs. French has been through, and is still going through, a period of suffering; hence her nerves are unstrung, and you make every allowance for her petulant phrases. You refer to back letters and look up the excuses she made for delay in the past months, and find they were all reasonable on the face of them. You decide therefore this is a case for patience and diplomacy—the patience that does not take her pleas too seriously, and the displomacy that says it is best for her and for you that she begin to pay the debt in small amounts.

Dear Madam:

Your letter of the 17th was received and we desire at once to express our deep regret in learning of the illness of your daughter and of the costly operation it necessitated. We quite understand how this unexpected expenditure has made an inroad into your finances, but we wish to suggest that the best way out of the difficulty is to pay us a small sum weekly, say $5.00, until the debt is fully discharged.

You point out that we have a large business and we appreciate the remark; but we have grown because we have given the public the benefit of our buying large quantities of goods for cash, thus securing their confidence. Our monthly disbursements are very considerable, and it is therefore to our advantage (and to yours) that country store-keepers should pay promptly, otherwise we cannot offer them the same goods at the same prices.

Please write by return saying you will act on our suggestion.

Yours truly,
Bolt & Co.

The man who *can* pay and *won't* should be handled discreetly but firmly. He often boasts to others that he never pays until he is forced to do so; he "allows the money to lie in the bank and gain interest." Sometimes his vanity is tickled by an office salesman who, in writing to him, says, "it is well known you are a man of means and therefore you ought to send your check." But these compliments lose their force after a time and the debtor hardens his heart. To get the money you must be businesslike and tell him exactly what you are going to do.

Dear Sir:

Your account with us is now two months overdue, and we wish to inform you that unless it is paid within two days, our attorney will enter suit for the $50.00, together with legal costs of the action. Further, we have decided that unless you have some reasonable explanation of this delay to offer, all dealings with us in the future will be on a cash basis.

Yours truly,
Bolt & Co.

The debtor will no doubt pay immediately, because he does not want an exposure, but mainly because the gain effected by keeping his money in the bank is one he prizes highly, and this gain, though small, can only come by means of a credit account.

EXERCISES

A. QUESTIONS FOR REVIEW:
  (1) Name the three kinds of letters usually sent out to people who are slow in making their payments.
  (2) Does the office salesman take into account the circumstances of the debtor in pressing for a remittance?
  (3) How is the wilful debtor handled?

B. QUESTIONS FOR WRITTEN ANSWERS:
  (1) To John H. Goschalk, who is running a store at Waslyn, a little town in Ohio, write a letter requesting a remittance of $30. He is often behind time and is now one month overdue. His great excuse has always been the dwindling population and poor trade.
  (2) Write a letter to Arthur Mason of North Chicago, requesting payment of $10.00 in 24 hours or the matter will be handled by your attorney. You have private information that his finances are in a shaky condition.

LESSON FORTY-EIGHT
"Don'ts" for Office Salesmen

THE first is *"Don't despise details."* It is no trifle to allow a smudged letter to leave the office, or one that has an incorrect address; it is not unimportant to leave out a comma, or to allow the expression, "same shall have our attention" instead of "your request has had our attention," or some other rendering.

Apart from the guiding principles already noticed, successful letter writing depends on the observance of detail. For instance, you should use good stationery. Don't use inferior because it is cheap. That course is just as absurd as if a commercial traveller dressed himself in rough clothing because he thereby saved a few dollars. He knows how much depends on a good appearance and he spends his money accordingly.

Now your office stationery is to you what good clothes are to the outside salesman; and as you are taking much care with your words and phrases don't send them out in shabby and cheap attire.

Again, *don't crowd your letters.* Give each argument a brief paragraph, then break off, thus affording it room to breathe and assert its individuality. Next begin a new paragraph and continue the method until you come to the last. Aim at a balanced letter, by which I mean that its proportions shall be in harmony. Below is a sort of shadow sketch of what I intend:

```
_____ Heading _____
                                                _____ Date
Name
      Address
Salutation
_____
_____ 1st paragraph _____
_____
_____ 2d paragraph _____
                    (Subscription)
                                          _____ (Signature)
```

A moment ago I argued on behalf of good stationery because it is equivalent to good clothes. But you may have good clothes and not know how to put them on. So don't forget the art of learning how to "dress" a letter.

Don't write to women buyers in exactly the same way as you would to men buyers.

A woman is always prepared for twice as much detail, and is ready to spend twice the amount of time, in making her purchases, consequently you have less need to stint the length of your replies, especially answers to inquiry letters. As between a brief and extremely "businesslike" answer, and one that conveys the same information in a more chatty manner, a woman will always follow the latter, because, being naturally more of an artist than a man, she will take more pains in selection and arrangement.

As in most countries women buyers exceed men buyers in numbers, it is important that office salesmen should not forget this difference in viewpoint. An observance of it is right in itself, because it gives greater service and creates deeper confidence, and service is the source of profit.

Another "Don't," commonplace no doubt, but important, is *Don't be careless in matters of postage.*

There are customers who think nothing about losing a dollar, but who will bitterly resent having to pay two cents extra postage on a letter of yours, even though it be in reply to one of theirs. Always bear in mind that the postage stamp conscience has a separate compartment in every person's brain, and *that* conscience regards an unstamped envelope as a grievous crime even though it contains a check and the mail carrier only wants two cents for it. Absurd logic it may be, but it is a fact; just as it is a complementary fact that to receive a stamped and addressed envelope is regarded as "very kind and thoughtful."

Further, if a correspondent asks to be addressed in plain envelopes, oblige him, not once but always. There are peculiarly sensitive people in the world and it is just as well to accommodate yourself to their peculiarities.

Don't believe you have reached a finality of excellence. There is a disposition even among very successful men to imagine they have reached the summit of perfection in methods of selling, and that anybody coming after them would be compelled to adopt the same methods.

And there is a similar disposition in the minds of the partially successful but it arises out of their failure to do what they intended to do. They believe, despairingly, that they have tried everything and nothing else remains to be done or to be done better.

It is always wise to believe "the best is yet to be" even in salesmanship. Excellence seldom knows finality; the way is ever open to improvement. Do not therefore close the door of your mind and refuse to admit the possibility of a new selling idea. Keep the door open night and day, and the thought you have long waited for will come, unexpectedly perhaps, but surely.

EXERCISES

A. QUESTIONS FOR REVIEW:
  (1) Are there any *trifles* in salesmanship?
  (2) What are the "Don'ts" of the preceding lesson?
  (3) Why is it wise to believe in the possibility of "a better way?"

B. QUESTIONS FOR WRITTEN ANSWERS:
  (1) What should be the policy in writing letters to women buyers? Justify your answer.
  (2) "There is the positive good, the comparative better and the superlative best. But we ought never to say we have reached the superlative degree." Why is that so?

H
SELLING BY ADVERTISEMENT

LESSON FORTY-NINE

SALESMANSHIP AND ADVERTISING

IT has been said that "advertising is salesmanship on paper," a definition which, though not wholly true, is true enough to indicate the fact that advertising is a branch of selling.

A salesman, whether wholesale, retail, or specialty, generally appeals to one person: an office salesman appeals to thousands at the same time, and he may do it by letter and circular—like the promoter—or through the advertising space of a newspaper or other journal.

In any case, the underlying principles are those we have discussed in previous lessons: an advertisement writer sits down to appeal to human desire and to stimulate a decision to buy; and he does it by arresting attention and creating interest.

He arrests attention by some striking phrase set up in type that will catch the eye, or by some design that discharges the same function. Having caught the reader's eye and secured his attention, he prepares a few phrases that are sure to create interest, compelling the reader to read on. The next step is to insure that his interest will pass into desire and desire into action.

Thus it is evident that, although an advertisement may seldom be regarded by the public as a selling talk, it *is* one nevertheless, and sometimes approaches a very high standard of excellence. And the more consistently it obeys the mental law of sale the more certain is it to be a successful appeal to the reader.

The salesman who has the advantage of being connected with a firm that spends money in advertising should regard the expenditure as a help towards his own efforts; not, as some do, as a competitive force rendering the work of the traveller unnecessary. To argue that goods which can be sold by advertising need no personal canvass is to miss the point: a clever salesman presses this expenditure into his list of arguments and makes it an additional reason for the buyer to buy. Goods worth so much advertising must be good goods.

Again, the salesman may contribute valuable information to the advertising department. That department knows the goods and it knows the art of telling an attractive story about them, but it does not know, until an outsider brings the news, what the customer is saying about them. And it is important not only to know but to act upon these news items. If the general impression about a new sewing machine is that it differs little from prevailing types, the advertising department is very glad to make use of such an impression and spares no pains to correct it in the ads that are being prepared. The salesman and the publicity department can thus work together.

The former, instead of feeling that his occupation is gone because the firm's ads are "pulling" orders, realizes that his work is made more responsible, for the firm looks to him to make their advertising investment more certain of a secure return.

EXERCISES

A. QUESTIONS FOR REVIEW:
  (1) How is the advertisement writer a salesman?
  (2) In what way does he fulfil the mental law of sale?
  (3) What is the possible useful connection between a salesman and the advertising department?

B. QUESTIONS FOR WRITTEN ANSWERS:
  (1) Show how advertising is a benefit to the salesman.
  (2) What is the function of art in advertising?

I
CONCLUDING SURVEY

LESSON FIFTY

SUGGESTIONS FOR FURTHER STUDY

IN this concluding lesson I wish to remind you of the main truths which have been dealt with in the preceding pages, and to offer suggestions for further study.

So many aspects of salesmanship have been investigated that it may seem impossible to codify them in one brief lesson; but this is not so. Everything I have said has to do with one of four topics:

1. Know yourself;
2. Know the customer;
3. Know the goods;
4. Apply that knowledge.

Take any page you like and you will find that the ideas under review can be included under one of these four headings. This fact simplifies the method to be adopted for the revision of past lessons, and provides an outline for more advanced study.

Much has been said about the work of preparation which the salesman must go through before he is truly efficient, but there is still much that has not even been referred to. He is called upon to develop his bodily and mental powers, thereby obtaining a physique with enduring qualities, and a mind characterized by growing ability, originality and force. Mind is divided into three sections: knowing, feeling and willing. Each section can be cultivated to a high pitch of excellence, and excellence is a synonym for success. Memory, imagination, concentration, honesty and will power are only a few of the qualities of mind that demand attention if a salesman would educate himself for a high-grade position.

Turning to the study of the customer—which is really the study of human nature—we see how vast a subject is revealed for character analysis. To be able to know what the differences are between man and man, and to know why they exist and what they imply is knowledge that has a great commercial value; it prevents mistakes in approaching a customer, it provides a key to unlock the door of a stranger's temperament, and it decides the manner in which we unfold the selling talk.

Supplementary to the lessons on analyzing the goods is the need of applying psychology to the arrangement of the points brought out in the analysis—a fine study in the details of an article as they are related to the needs of the public and the constitution of the mind. Moreover, the term "goods" includes all items of cost, of office systems, and of display, each of which requires separate treatment.

The fourth point, the *use* of the knowledge gained, is the sum total of salesmanship: it reduces to practice, and justifies the program of study that has gone before. And, although this text book confines itself to the art of selling, it can be said to have touched only the fringe of the subject: there are a hundred and one details calling for notice, not one of which can be called unimportant. Still the student may rest assured that he has now a firm hold of the elementary principles of salesmanship, and his enthusiasm being aroused, it is now my duty to show him the way to more advanced work.

The vocation of a salesman demands a course of training quite as much as do the duties of a physician. The past lessons cover the practice of selling; they constitute to the young salesman what "walking the hospitals" means to the young medical student. But walking a hospital does not make a capable physician; he must study physiology, anatomy, medicines, chemistry and many other things. And lessons in selling will not make a youth all he wants to be as a salesman; he has to study his own character, the physiology and chemistry of human nature, the complete why and wherefore of the articles he disposes of, and acquire the gifts of skill in applying that knowledge.

These facts are urged upon you to show the dignity and power of the salesman's occupation. You take your place with the best of the skilled professions, and yield to none in the intricacy of your curriculum of studies, whilst the financial rewards are higher than in any other professional sphere.

The course of training outlined in this lesson is contained in the Science of Business-building in 32 volumes, and inquiries respecting tuition may be addressed to the author at the Sheldon University Press, Libertyville, Ill.

EXERCISES

A. QUESTIONS FOR REVIEW:
  (1) What four topics summarize the thoughts of all the preceding lessons?
  (2) Describe the program for individual self culture.
  (3) How would you increase your knowledge of (a) the goods, and (b) the customer?

B. QUESTIONS FOR WRITTEN ANSWERS:
  (1) Unfold the advantages of being able to read character at a glance.
  (2) Since all business is salesmanship in essence, show how an increased knowledge of the goods includes their material and manufacture under the most economical conditions.